AND
SARAH
SAW

AND SARAH SAW

FRANCES SWAGGART

JIMMY SWAGGART MINISTRIES
P.O. Box 262550 | Baton Rouge, Louisiana 70826-2550
www.jsm.org

ISBN 978-1-941403-25-9
09-136 | COPYRIGHT © 2016 Jimmy Swaggart Ministries®
16 17 18 19 20 21 22 23 24 25/ BVG / 10 9 8 7 6 5 4 3 2 1

TABLE OF CONTENTS

AND SARAH SAW

PREFACE

PREFACE

"WOE UNTO THEM THAT call evil good, and good evil; that put darkness for light, and light for darkness; that put bitter for sweet, and sweet for bitter" (Isaiah 5:20).

I see this world in a very dangerous and precarious situation right now. Things are not looking as good as they should in this country and in other countries around the world. The world needs the Lord Jesus Christ. He is the answer to all of the problems that we see unfolding — trends that are quite alarming: horrific acts of terrorism, the national debt now in the trillions, immigration, gun violence; the list goes on and on.

These trends are symptoms of the great compromise in our country — America's God-given freedoms and values diluted with ungodly agendas created by ungodly leaders. We've reached a point in this country where American citizens can no longer tell the difference between what is good and what is evil.

Sadly, the majority of the church is also confused. Never before has there been a time when spiritual discernment is so lacking in the body of Christ than it is today.

When faced with issues that threaten our freedoms, our safety, and most of all, our faith, we have Christians who are buckling under social and political pressures to go along with the way of the world. They tolerate the evil happening around them and defend that stance to other Christians by calling their compromise *compassion*.

Love, they say. Turn the other cheek, they say. And of course, as Christians we love people. But we show that love by sharing the gospel with them. As for turning the other cheek, remember how the Lord responded when He was struck by an officer for teaching the truth:

> *"The high priest then asked Jesus of his disciples, and of his doctrine. Jesus answered him, I spake openly to the world; I ever taught in the synagogue, and in the temple, whither the Jews always resort; and in secret have I said nothing. Why askest thou me? ask them which heard me, what I have said unto them: behold, they know what I said. And when he had thus spoken, one of the officers which stood by struck Jesus with the palm of his hand, saying, Answerest thou the high priest so? Jesus answered him, If I have spoken evil, bear witness of the evil: but if well, why smitest thou me?"* (John 18:19-23).

This is where the church is at today, hitting those who dare to speak out against evil with words of mockery.

Christians have traded wisdom and the Word of God for false doctrines taught by hirelings.

Christian leadership today is all but gone. The individual believer is now responsible for discerning right from wrong, truth from deception, and the Word of God from another gospel. God gives the Christian wisdom, knowledge, and discernment, which are beautiful gifts. But we're not using those today.

Christians must open their eyes and stop believing all of this false trash that is coming into the church today. It is a mockery of God, and I feel like I'm very inadequate in making you understand just how serious the situation is.

As a Christian, you must see the world through the eyes of the Bible and judge everything according to the Scriptures. Whether the problem is political, economical, social, or educational, everything must be looked at through the lens of God's Word.

That's why my husband and I felt it was so important to make a book of these hand-selected articles from recent issues of *The Evangelist*.

You are about to read a collection of 25 articles published in *The Evangelist* magazine from 2008 to 2016. All articles were re-edited for corrections in grammar, usage, and style. References specific to the original publication date of each article have been modified or removed. Also, some of the original titles were shortened or changed, but all original article titles and their publication dates are listed in the references section in the back of the book.

Each chapter confronts a current issue that is rapidly changing the church and the country and provides Scriptures that address each topic.

After 60 years of ministry, my husband and I know that in order for the Word of God to work in the hearts and lives of people, the truth has got to be spoken out. And we love you enough to tell you the truth.

Our prayer for you is that you love the Lord Jesus Christ enough to accept the truth and stand up for Him in these last days.

As I mentioned before, this world is in a very dangerous and precarious situation. But thank God for all that He is doing to uphold the freedoms that we still have in the United States of America so that the gospel of the Lord Jesus Christ can be preached to the whole world.

Frances Swaggart
— 2016 —

AND SARAH SAW

CHAPTER 1

AND SARAH SAW

AND SARAH SAW

AND SARAH SAW THE son of Hagar the Egyptian, which she had born unto Abraham, mocking. Wherefore she said unto Abraham, Cast out this bondwoman and her son: for the son of this bondwoman shall not be heir with my son, even with Isaac. And the thing was very grievous in Abraham's sight because of his son. And God said unto Abraham, Let it not be grievous in thy sight because of the lad, and because of thy bondwoman; in all that Sarah hath said unto thee, hearken unto her voice; for in Isaac shall thy seed be called (Gen. 21:9-12).

An email I received and read on *Frances & Friends* compared this complex situation between Abraham, Sarah, and Isaac, and Hagar and Ishmael to the Syrian refugees now living among us in the United States of America.

In the book of Genesis, Sarah sees Ishmael mocking. This was an ongoing problem that was never going to stop. Ishmael — a work of the flesh — could not continue to co-exist with Isaac — a work of the Spirit. Had Sarah not voiced her concern to Abraham, it is quite possible that Ishmael's mocking would have resulted in the murder of their promise child, Isaac.

Consider these notes regarding Ishmael and Isaac from my husband's Bible commentary:

> *'But as then he that was born after the flesh perse-cuted him that was born after the spirit, even so it is now'* (Gal. 4:29). Paul is referring to an incident in Genesis Chapter 21. Isaac is being weaned. It is possible that he was upward of 5 years old, and if so, Ishmael would have been about 19. (In Gen. 21:9) the implication is that Ishmael was mocking Isaac and possibly Sarah as well. As Paul describes in Galatians 4:29, the word persecuted is understood by some Greek scholars as to imply murder. And Scripture confirms it. In other words, Ishmael hated Isaac, and actually wanted to murder him. This was why Sarah asked that Hagar and her son be sent away.

Praise the Lord, Sarah did speak up. Since the life of her only son was at stake, she did not mince words. Neither was Sarah concerned about being politically correct when she told Abraham, *"Cast out this bondwoman and her son."*

Of course the situation was a very painful one for Abraham because Ishmael was his son. Surely it was an extremely difficult decision for him to make and to follow through by sending Ishmael and his mother out from under his care and protection. But he listened to Sarah — as the Lord told him to do — and Abraham obeyed God.

I do see a correlation between this truth from Genesis and the Muslim refugees who live among us in the United States of America.

My question is this: Can Muslims and Christians continue to co-exist in this country? Ishmael and Isaac reached a point where they could not.

Every day the media reports evidence of growing tensions between Islam and Christianity. As the Muslim community grows in America, so does its desire to dominate in our schools, cities, and government.

THE CURRENT SITUATION

President Obama decided that America will become the new and permanent home for 10,000 Syrian refugees in FY16 — a number that is expected to increase. Nearly 1,500 are already here. The U.S. will accept 85,000 refugees from around the world in 2016 and 100,000 in 2017, according to Secretary of State John Kerry.

The president's decision did not require congressional approval and was apparently made without discussion of alternatives to migration, such as assisting the refugees in camps nearest to their homelands. There seems to be an agenda in place to uproot these people and force them into the European Union, with increasing pressure on the U.S. to take in its fair share.

America was even admonished on the issue by Pope Francis who spoke to Congress from his temporary U.S.

pulpit: "We need to avoid a common temptation nowadays: to discard whatever proves troublesome."

That's an odd statement to make to a country that has given so much in humanitarian aid to countries in crisis. Syria has been no exception.

From FY12 to FY15, the U.S. government has given more than $4.5 billion in assistance to the Syrian humanitarian response, according to the agency primarily responsible for administering civilian foreign aid — the United States Agency for International Development.

In addition to these billions of U.S. dollars already spent, the United Nations is still pressing America to open her borders wider and take in more refugees, whose total population rivals the migrations of World War II.

In September, *Time Magazine* reported this:

"Since the Syrian Civil War began in March 2011, 1,584 refugees have been relocated in the U.S., the majority of whom have moved to Texas (180), California (171), Michigan (159), Illinois (132), Arizona (107) and Florida (97). Thirty other states have absorbed the rest, according to numbers compiled by the State Department."

Although often used interchangeably, let me define the two terms *refugee* and *immigrant*. A refugee is someone who has been forced to leave a country because of war or for religious or political reasons. An immigrant is a person who comes to a country to take up *permanent* residence.

The refugees already here, plus the 10,000 Syrians coming now, plan to make the U.S. their permanent residence.

THE CONCERN

For Christians and other conservatives, the primary concern around this intake of Syrian refugees is that Islamic terrorists will infiltrate this ongoing migration and slip through undetected into the United States.

Rep. Peter King (R-NY), chairman of the House Subcommittee on Counterterrorism and Intelligence, shares this concern. In September he told CNN, "We have to assume that ISIS or al Qaeda would try to take advantage of this situation."

According to its website, the Counterterrorism and Intelligence Subcommittee "focuses on the capabilities and efforts of the Federal government, particularly the Department of Homeland Security, to identify and deter threats to the Homeland through the collection and sharing of counterterrorism and homeland security information across Federal, State, and local law enforcement."

Congressman King, the man who heads this subcommittee, describes ISIS this way:

> ISIS is a vicious jihadist terrorist organization which continues to make advances in large parts of Iraq and Syria. ISIS in the Middle East today is stronger than Al Qaeda was in Afghanistan in 2001. It is far wealthier and battle-hardened than Osama Bin Laden's henchmen. ISIS includes Americans in its ranks, and is actively trying to recruit more via social media. ISIS has demonstrated its depraved, evil and barbaric nature toward Americans by

killing aid worker Kayla Mueller, beheading journalists James Foley, Steven Sotloff, and former U.S. Army Ranger Peter Kassig.

In 2015 over 50 individuals have been arrested in the United States for their connections to ISIS. Many of these individuals were apprehended while planning attacks on New York, including Abdurasul Juraboev, Khror Saidakhmetov, Abror Habibov, Dilkhayot Kasimov and Akmal Zakirov who had planned to travel to Syria and join ISIS, bomb Coney Island, kill members of the NYPD and the President; Samuel Rahamin Topaz, Munther Omar Saleh, Fareed Mumuni, Alaa Saadeh, Nader Saadeh who, along with an unnamed minor, planned to attack various landmarks throughout New York City and provide material support to ISIS; and Noelle Velentzas and Asia Siddiqui, who were planning to attack a large law-enforcement event, like a funeral for a member of the NYPD.

Yet King's concern, and the concern of so many others, goes unheeded by President Obama who will not even speak the words, "Islamic extremism."

Neil Macdonald of CBC News said it well:

Why Obama and some other Western leaders frame their rhetoric that way is obvious. They want to shield law-abiding Muslim citizens from popular anger as provocations grow more atrocious by the month. Plus, they are anxious to repudiate any idea of a war between the largely Christian West and the Islamic world.

But that is the way ISIS and its fellow travelers see things, and those atrocities — the immolation of the Jordanian pilot in the name of Allah, the Internet videos of hooded figures hacking the heads off Western hostages in the name of Allah, the slaughter at a French magazine in the name of Allah — are having the desired effect.

It's pretty safe to say that in the broad public mind, both here and in Europe, Islam is not synonymous with peace.

I could add to this list the recent crucifixion of a 12-year-old boy who refused to deny his faith in the Lord Jesus Christ.

Ladies and gentlemen, these are just more of the realities — the results — of true Islam. Yet even after hearing and seeing these cruelties, many still hold to an unrealistic view of the Muslim religion, calling it a religion of peace and love when we see example after example of the complete opposite.

The angel of the Lord told Hagar how Ishmael would be:

'And he will be a wild man; his hand will be against every man, and every man's hand against him; and he shall dwell in the presence of all his brethren.'

(These predictions describe the Arab people perfectly. They cannot get along with anyone in the world, and they cannot even get along among themselves. The descendants of Ishmael dwell in the presence of all his brethren [Israel], but do not subdue them and,

in fact, never will subdue them!) (Gen. 16:12, The
Expositor's Study Bible).

NO LONGER THE MINORITY?

America was founded on Christian principles and values, which included religious freedom. As a Christian nation,
America is a compassionate nation and has welcomed others
seeking such freedom.

For the past 240 years, Christian America has grown
up peaceably with other religions in its midst including
Buddhism, Catholicism, Hinduism, Jehovah's Witness,
and Mormonism. While these other religions disagree in
doctrine, none pose any danger.

It's not so with Islam. As the religion of Islam matures in
the United States, we are experiencing the same problems
that Sarah saw regarding Hagar and Ishmael — mocking and
demanding, with a desire for murder.

School boards in America have been pressured by
Muslim community leaders to eliminate references to all
religious holidays — Christmas and Easter — on calendars
and close public schools in observance of the Muslim holy
day, Eid al-Adha.

When a New Jersey school board told Muslim parents
that its schools would remain open on Eid al-Adha, Muslim
families were outraged. *The Daily Mail* reported that a
woman wearing a headscarf took a microphone during the
meeting and told the school board panel, "We're no longer

the minority, that's clear from tonight. We're going to be the majority *soon*."

Middle school students in Tennessee were required to recite and write the words, "Allah is the only god," as part of their history project on the Five Pillars of Islam. One parent told Fox News, "It really did bother me that they skipped the whole chapter on the rise of Christianity and they spent three weeks just studying Islam."

When presidential candidate Dr. Ben Carson said he would not support a Muslim for president if that person refused to put the U.S. Constitution above the tenets of Islam, his comments were called "anti-Muslim."

Yet, when Fox News interviewed Muslim men on the streets of New York and asked them if sharia law should supersede the U.S. Constitution, one Muslim said this: "The U.S. Constitution is made by people and the sharia law is made by Allah, so that [sharia] is all the way above, that has to be definitely in the land not for the America but for the whole world, would be above."

THE COMPLAINT

As America takes in more and more Muslims, we should expect to experience the same problem that England and France is facing: a refusal by Muslims to assimilate in countries where they now live.

In the U.K., Muslims now make up 5 percent of the entire population, and Islam is its second largest religion.

They have moved past the point of Muslim influence in their communities and schools.

Although still disconnecting the religion of Islam from Islamist terrorism, European leaders hosting large Muslim populations cannot deny and must now deal with an escalation in violence.

Six months ago, British Prime Minister David Cameron outlined a new strategy to prevent Islamist extremism in a speech to the Ninestiles School in Birmingham.

> It begins — it must begin — by understanding the threat we face and why we face it. What we are fighting, in Islamist extremism, is an ideology. It is an extreme doctrine. And like any extreme doctrine, it is subversive. At its furthest end it seeks to destroy nation-states to invent its own barbaric realm. And it often backs violence to achieve this aim — mostly violence against fellow Muslims — who don't subscribe to its sick worldview.

In his speech, Cameron admitted a lack of confidence to enforce Britain's values for fear of causing offense.

> The failure in the past to confront the horrors of forced marriage I view as a case in point. So is the utter brutality of Female Genital Mutilation (FGM). It sickens me to think that there were nearly 4,000 cases of FGM reported in our country last year alone. Four thousand cases; think about that. And 11,000 cases of so-called honour-based violence over the last 5 years — and that's just the reported cases.

Unfortunately, the president of the United States is unwilling to connect the realities of Islam to its terroristic agenda.

Just 45 days after two Islamist gunmen killed 12 people at the Paris headquarters of the French satirical weekly magazine *Charlie Hebdo,* President Obama spoke to an audience represented by more than 60 countries at the summit on "Countering Violent Extremism."

After listing recent cruelties carried out by the Islamic State of Iraq and Syria in the Middle East, Canada, Australia, France, and Denmark, President Obama made this statement:

"We have to confront the warped ideologies espoused by terrorists like al Qaeda and ISIL, especially their attempt to use Islam to justify their violence. I discussed this at length yesterday. These terrorists are desperate for legitimacy. And all of us have a responsibility to refute the notion that groups like ISIL somehow represent Islam, because that is a falsehood that embraces the terrorist narrative."

This is no falsehood, Mr. President. To the families who have watched or read the horrifying details of how their loved ones were murdered by Islamists, the truth about Islam is very real.

CONCLUSION

To allow people into the United States or Europe who are clearly against the established form of government and the

freedoms these countries uphold is detrimental and dangerous to our country and to our way of life.

Sadly, the decision to let more refugees into America has
already been made. Once again, Ishmael is in the same camp
with Isaac.

As Christians, we must open our eyes and see, just as
Sarah saw, and look at Islam for exactly what it is. Then, as
Sarah did to Abraham, we need to speak up, ask questions,
and voice our concerns about the threats Islam poses to our
country.

Do the Muslims living in the United States show a love
for the American people? I don't see that happening. Are
these refugees, whom we are spending so much money to
help, feed, protect, and bring into this country, appreciative
or thankful for what America is doing for them? These are
serious questions to consider.

Above all, we must continually pray for our country.
Donnie said it right the other day: "We are in a spiritual fight
for the soul of our nation."

AND SARAH SAW

CHAPTER 2

AMERICA IS NOT A MUSLIM NATION

AMERICA IS NOT A MUSLIM NATION

BECAUSE SENTENCE AGAINST AN evil work is not executed speedily, therefore the heart of the sons of men is fully set in them to do evil (Eccl. 8:11).

As a young student in school, I can remember studying about the Barbary Wars. Never in my wildest dreams could I have known that one day I would be standing and looking out over the Atlantic Ocean as our host pointed out the trade route that many of the merchant ships would take, always concerned that pirates could slip aboard at night, take over the ship and its crew, and hold them for ransom.

At issue was the Barbary pirates' demand for tribute from merchant vessels. If ships of a given country failed to pay, Muslim pirates would attack the ships and take their goods, and often enslave their crewmembers or hold them for ransom.

When I heard our president make the statement that "The United States was one of the largest Muslim nations in the world," my mind immediately went back to the Barbary Wars.

Two hundred years ago, the United States declared war

on Islam. Thomas Jefferson was president at the time, and he refused to pay tribute to the Islamic pirates. He sent a United States naval fleet to the Mediterranean; bombarding their various fortified pirate cities, ultimately extracting concessions of fair passage from their rulers. This took place between 1801 and 1805. In 1815, President James Madison had to undertake the very same actions again. Those pirate cities are what we know now today as Libya, Tunisia, and Algeria.

AN EMAIL WORTH READING

After mentioning the Barbary Wars on a recent episode of *Frances & Friends,* I received the following email from one of our listeners. The fact that the information in this email has shown up in multiple articles, blogs, and elsewhere proves that people are extremely interested in America's response to the problem of Islamic terrorism.

You will see how the response, especially from former U.S. presidents, was then compared to what our president says today. As you read this, I think you will agree with me that the United States is not, nor has it ever been, a Muslim nation. The email reads:

> At the height of the eighteenth century, Muslim pirates were the terror of the Mediterranean and a large area of the North Atlantic. They attacked every ship in sight, and held the crews for exorbitant ransoms. Those taken hostage were subjected to barbaric treatment and wrote heartbreaking letters home, begging their government

and family members to pay whatever their Mohammedan captors demanded.

These extortionists of the high seas represented the Islamic nations of Tripoli, Tunis, Morocco, and Algiers — collectively referred to as the Barbary Coast — and presented a dangerous and unprovoked threat to the new American Republic.

Before the Revolutionary War, U.S. merchant ships had been under the protection of Great Britain. When the U.S. declared its independence and entered into war, the ships of the United States were protected by France. However, once the war was won, America had to protect its own fleets. Thus, the birth of the U.S. Navy.

Beginning in 1784, 17 years before he would become president, Thomas Jefferson became America's minister to France. That same year, the U.S. Congress sought to appease its Muslim adversaries by following in the footsteps of European nations who paid bribes to the Barbary States, rather than engaging them in war.

In July of 1785, Algerian pirates captured American ships, and the Dey of Algiers demanded an unheard-of ransom of $60,000. It was a plain and simple case of extortion, and Thomas Jefferson was vehemently opposed to any further payments. Instead, he proposed to Congress the formation of a coalition of allied nations who together could force the Islamic states into peace. A disinterested Congress decided to pay the ransom.

In 1786, Thomas Jefferson and John Adams met with Tripoli's ambassador to Great Britain to ask by what right his nation attacked American ships and enslaved American citizens, and why Muslims held so much hostility towards America, a nation with which they had no previous contacts.

The two future presidents reported that Ambassador Sidi Haji Abdul Rahman Adja had answered that Islam was founded on the laws of their Prophet, that it was written in their Quran, that all nations who should not have acknowledged their authority were sinners, that it was their right and duty to make war upon them wherever they could be found, and to make slaves of all they could take as prisoners, and that every Mussulman (Muslim) who should be slain in battle was sure to go to paradise.

Despite of this stunning admission of premeditated violence on non-Muslim nations, as well as the objections of many notable American leaders, including George Washington, who warned that caving in was both wrong and would only further embolden the enemy, for the following 15 years, the American government paid the Muslims millions of dollars for the safe passage of American ships or the return of American hostages. The payments in ransom and tribute amounted to over 20 percent of the United States government annual revenues in 1800.

Jefferson was disgusted. Shortly after his being sworn in as the third president of the United States in 1801, the pasha of Tripoli sent him a note demanding the immediate payment of $225,000 plus $25,000 a year for every year forthcoming. That changed everything.

Jefferson let the pasha know, in no uncertain terms, what he could do with his demand. The pasha responded by cutting down the flagpole at the American consulate and declared war on the United States. Tunis, Morocco, and Algiers immediately followed suit. Jefferson, until now, had been against America raising a naval force for anything beyond coastal defense, but having watched his nation be cowed by Islamic thuggery for long enough, decided that is was finally time to meet force with force.

He dispatched a squadron of frigates to the Mediterranean and taught the Muslim nations of the Barbary Coast a lesson he hoped they would never forget. Congress authorized Jefferson to empower U.S. ships to seize all vessels and goods of the pasha of Tripoli and to 'cause to be done all other acts of precaution or hostility as the state of war would justify.'

When Algiers and Tunis, who were both accustomed to American cowardice and acquiescence, saw the newly independent United States had both the will and the might to strike back, they quickly abandoned their allegiance to Tripoli. The war with Tripoli lasted for four more years, and raged up again in 1815. The bravery of the U.S. Marine Corps in these wars led to the line 'to the shores of Tripoli' in the Marines' Hymn. They would forever be known as 'leathernecks' for the leather collars of their uniforms, designed to prevent their heads from being cut off by the Muslim scimitars when boarding enemy ships.

Islam, and what its Barbary followers justified doing in the name of their prophet and their god, disturbed Jefferson quite deeply. America had a tradition of religious tolerance, the fact that Jefferson, himself, had co-authored the Virginia Statute for Religious Freedom, but fundamentalist Islam was like no other religion the world had ever seen. A religion based on supremacism, whose holy book not only condoned but mandated violence against unbelievers was unacceptable to him. His greatest fear was that someday this brand of Islam would return and pose an even greater threat to the United States.

This should bother every American. That the Islams have brought about women-only classes and swimming times at taxpayer-funded universities and public pools; that Christians, Jews, and Hindus have been banned from serving on juries where Muslim defendants are being judged, Piggy banks and Porky Pig tissue dispensers have been banned from workplaces because they offend Islamist sensibilities. Ice cream has been discontinued at certain Burger King locations because the picture on the wrapper looks similar to the Arabic script for Allah, public schools are pulling pork from their menus, on and on in the newspapers.

It's death by a thousand cuts, or inch-by-inch as some refer to it, and most Americans have no idea that this battle is being waged every day across America. By not fighting back, by allowing groups to obfuscate what is really happening, and not insisting that the Islamists adapt to our own culture, the United States is cutting its own throat with a politically correct knife, and helping to further the Islamists agenda. Sadly, it appears that today's America would rather be politically correct than victorious.

The information in this email has been researched and found to be true. Still, I would encourage you to check the facts yourself.

THEN VERSUS NOW

History clearly shows how U.S. presidents Jefferson and Madison reacted to terrorism more than 200 years ago. Yet how do their responses then compare to statements today made by President Obama regarding the acceleration of Islamic terrorism happening in the world today?

I hope Americans are listening to what I'm about to state: America is waking up to a totally different and dangerous world than what this generation has ever seen. I feel like America is in a very precarious situation because we have unleashed a religion that is not going to stop until it conquers every continent, every nation, every country, and every little city and village in the world.

Recently, the news media also seems to be waking up to the realities of Islam as journalists report on terrorist activities and attacks which are more violent and happening more frequently in various parts of the world. As I write this article, we've seen five terrorist attacks in just as many months — all linked to Islamic terrorism:

Sept. 25, 2014: Islam convert, Alton Nolen, beheads one coworker and stabs a second at a food processing plant in Moore, Oklahoma.

Oct. 22, 2014: Islam convert, Michael Zehaf-Bibeau, fatally shoots a security officer and then opens fire inside Parliament Hill in Ottawa, Canada.

Oct. 23, 2014: Islam convert, Zale H. Thompson, attacks a group of New York City police officers with a hatchet in broad daylight.

Dec. 15, 2014: Islamist Man Haron Monis, takes 17 people hostage at a café in Sydney Australia. Two of the hostages died.

Jan. 7, 2015: Islamist gunmen kill 12 people in the offices of the satirical newspaper, Charlie Hebdo in Paris, France.

The January attack in Paris renewed media attention and interest to the fact that France has the largest number of Muslims in Western Europe — roughly 10 percent of its population.

Such demographics may explain French President Francois Hollande's refusal to link terrorists in the Jan. 7 attack on his country to Islam, instead calling them "fanatics who have nothing to do with Islam."

He said this despite witness accounts of the gunmen shouting, "Allahu akbar!" (Allah is greater) and "We avenged the Prophet Muhammad!"

President Obama's response to the attack on Paris was also stripped of any connection between Islam and the terrorists, referring to the gunmen instead as "perpetrators" and "those who carry out senseless attacks" who will be ultimately forgotten. He described their actions as the "senseless violence of the few."

In a January panel hosted by Fox News, Robert Spencer, director of Jihad Watch, offered his opinion on why the White House avoids mentioning Islam.

"It seems as if the president thinks and the Administration thinks that if they say something is Islamic then they will be at war with the entire Islamic world and right-wing racist vigilantes will go and victimize innocent people in the United States," Spencer said. "Both are hogwash and nonsense and, what's happened is that we have effectively gotten ourselves into a position where it's forbidden to speak about the motives and goals of the enemy and you cannot possibly defeat an enemy that you refuse to understand."

In the same panel discussion, Brigitte Gabriel, founder and president of Act For America, said the Islamic Middle East does not tolerate any other faith or group of people.

"We minorities in the Middle East have been massacred, killed, my house was bombed; this is how I ended up in this country, as a refugee from the Middle East. It was happening when my parents were refugees when I was a child, newborn, and here I am in America today and my people are still fleeing because of the intolerance of Islamic extremism. So, my past is America's future unless America wakes up now and takes the necessary steps to protect itself."

Gabriel said those necessary steps include identifying the enemy by name in order to devise the strategy to defeat it.

She said, "Right now we have the president in the White House who doesn't have the moral clarity and the courage to stand up and say what we are fighting, and we need to do that in order for us to defeat this enemy. It is Islamic terrorism."

During a speech to the Henry Jackson Society in London, former Louisiana Governor Bobby Jindal declared, "Islam has a problem."

In his prepared remarks, Jindal went on to say this:

If Islam does not support what is happening in the name of Islam, then they need to stand up and stop it. Many Islamic leaders argue that these are the acts of a radical few. Ok, it is their problem, and they need to deal with it. Muslim leaders must make clear that anyone who commits acts of terror in the name of Islam is in fact not practicing Islam at all. If they refuse to say this, then they are condoning these acts of barbarism. There is no middle ground. Specifically, Muslim leaders need to condemn anyone who commits these acts of violence and clearly state that these people are evil and are enemies of Islam.

It's not enough to simply condemn violence, they must stand up and loudly proclaim that these people are not martyrs who will receive a reward in the afterlife, and rather they are murderers who are going to hell.

Ladies and gentlemen, the United States of America is not

a Muslim nation, it is a Christian nation, founded by leaders of faith in God and the Lord Jesus Christ.

As Christians, we must discern what our president and most political leaders refuse to see or talk about. And what we see happening is modern-day Islamic piracy killing and holding for ransom our American freedoms, and the tribute they want is not money, but our faith. Hear what I'm saying, church, and continue to pray for our nation.

AND SARAH SAW

CHAPTER 3

ENABLING EVIL

ENABLING EVIL

"OF THE NATIONS CONCERNING which the Lord said unto the children of Israel, Ye shall not go in to them, neither shall they come in unto you: for surely they will turn away your heart after their gods: Solomon clave unto these in love" (I Ki. 11:2).

When Solomon was about 20 years old, he was already the king of Israel and the Bible says his kingdom was "established greatly." The Scriptures tell us how Solomon loved the Lord, walked in the statutes of his father, David, and how he went to the great high place, Gibeon, to sacrifice a thousand burnt offerings upon the altar. It was in Gibeon that the Lord appeared to Solomon in a dream and told him, "Ask what shall I give you."

"And now, O Lord my God, Thou hast made Thy servant king instead of David my father: and I am but a little child: I know not how to go out or come in. And Thy servant is in the midst of Thy people which Thou hast chosen, a great people, that cannot be numbered nor counted for multitude. Give therefore Thy servant an understanding heart to judge Thy people, that I may discern between good and bad: for

who is able to judge this Thy so great a people?" (I Ki. 3:7-9)

His unselfish request pleased the Lord, and He gave Solomon a wise and understanding heart like no other before or after him. The Lord also gave the king what he didn't ask for: riches, honor, and the promise of long life — if Solomon walked in His ways.

Solomon's relationship with the Lord is demonstrated so beautifully in I Kings, Chapter 8, where we find the king over all of Israel praying in the temple that he built for the Lord:

"And Solomon stood before the altar of the LORD in the presence of all the congregation of Israel, and spread forth his hands toward heaven: And he said, LORD God of Israel, there is no God like Thee, in heaven above, or on earth beneath, who keepest covenant and mercy with Thy servants that walk before Thee with all their heart" (I Ki. 8:22-23).

Sadly, the story of Solomon darkens when he disobeys God by letting his love of influential foreign women to overshadow his covenant with the Lord. The Bible says that Solomon had 700 princess wives whom, Pulpit says in his commentary, "Were amassed for the purpose of amalgamating unions with other nations."

This indicates a shift in Solomon's faith for Israel's strength — from God to princesses with political power.

Despite God's command, Solomon brought his pagan wives and concubines into Israel perhaps with a false hope that they would forsake their religion and fear God as was his prayer for other strangers:

"Moreover concerning a stranger, that is not of Thy

people Israel, but cometh out of a far country for Thy name's sake; (For they shall hear of Thy great name, and of Thy strong hand, and of Thy stretched out arm;) when he shall come and pray toward this house; Hear Thou in heaven thy dwelling place, and do according to all that the stranger calleth to Thee for: that all people of the earth may know Thy name, to fear Thee, as do Thy people Israel; and that they may know that this house, which I have builded, is called by Thy name" (I Ki. 8:41-43).

But Solomon's foreign wives had no intention of forsaking their pagan worship. Instead, they demanded that Solomon build altars to worship their idols, which he did. Instead of turning his wives to the Lord, his wives turned Solomon's heart away from the Lord.

"And Solomon did evil in the sight of the LORD, *and went not fully after the* LORD, *as did David his father"* (I Ki. 11:6).

In his commentary on this passage from I Kings, my husband writes:

"There is no sadder picture in the Bible than that of Solomon's fall. His extraordinary gift of wisdom did not save him from disobedience to the law of God. His neglect of that law and his loss of fellowship with God, which gives power to it, opened the door wide to the entrance of every form of evil."

Solomon's decision to open Israel's borders to foreigners who were unwilling to assimilate proved to be unwise. America should take note because the president of the United States is making the same unwise decision.

Millions of refugees are pouring in from Syria into Europe and now the United States, and Americans are being pressured by the president and other world leaders to help these displaced people despite the national security threat of infiltration by terrorist groups.

President Obama went so far as to mock politicians who opposed his directive to welcome Syrian refugees into the U.S. and accused Republicans of being "scared of widows and orphans."

On November 13, 2015, when terrorists carried out the multi-sited attack on Paris and calmly gunned down 130 people while saying things like, "You need to think about Syria," President Obama still insisted that opening U.S. borders to Syrian refugees is the right thing to do and that the vetting process in place works. His plan is to resettle at least another 10,000 Syrian refugees into the U.S. in 2016.

Ladies and gentlemen, it is the primary responsibility of the president of the United States to keep the American people safe. But the actions of President Obama raise the question: Is he showing love to the people of America and to the refugees that he's trying to bring into this country, or is he enabling evil to flourish?

The people of France and Germany might be able to answer that question best. Their leaders agreed to open-border policies and are now dealing with a Muslim population of nearly 5 million in each country. In 2015, France alone experienced seven terrorist "incidents" mostly by Islamists — two mass shootings, three stabbings, and one beheading — that left a total of 152 people dead.

In addition to taking refugees into their country, Germany also has to house hundreds of thousands of "asylum-seekers" — more than 700,000 in 2015 — and pay them a stipend of $152 for basic needs.

Are these refugees thankful for the assistance? Are they assimilating? No, they are committing crimes. On Dec. 31, 2015, New Year's Eve, the following sexual assault cases involving refugees were reported in Germany, Switzerland, Sweden, and France:

> Cologne, Germany: As many as 1,000 men robbed and sexually assaulted (including rape) at least 120 women. Asylum-seekers from Syria were among the 32 suspects involved in this coordinated crime wave. The attackers have been described as of Arab or North African origin.

> Kalmar, Sweden: Fifteen women reported that they were groped by groups of men. Two men, both 'asylum-seekers,' are suspects.

> Switzerland: Police said six women were allegedly robbed and sexually assaulted. The women reported being surrounded by 'several dark-skinned men' who robbed, groped, and molested them.

> Helsinki, Finland: Security guards hired to patrol the capital city told police there was 'widespread sexual harassment.' The deputy police chief said, 'There hasn't been this kind of harassment on previous New Year's Eves, or other occasions for that matter... This is a completely new phenomenon.'

Ladies and gentlemen, what's happening as a result of this massive immigration is evil. Through his determination to bring 100,000 more refugees into this country over the next two years, President Obama is enabling more evil to happen in America.

Ecclesiastes 8:11 says, *"Because sentence against an evil work is not executed speedily, therefore the heart of the sons of men is fully set in them to do evil."*

Notes from my husband's commentary on this verse are excellent. They read:

"The government is morally and spiritually obligated to put down all 'evil work,' whether in the hearts and lives of individuals or in entire nations. To not do so will only increase the evil."

The scepter of world power is in the hands of the United States, where it has been almost from the beginning of the 20th century. This authority is given by God to this nation. America is responsible for several things:

- It is the God-given business of this nation to take the gospel of Jesus Christ to the ends of the earth. This doesn't mean that it is the government who will do this, but it does mean that government is to put no roadblocks or obstacles in the path of those who carry out the Great Commission. As someone has well said, "As long as the greatest export of the United States is the gospel of Jesus Christ, then the jackbooted heels of foreign invaders will never walk upon American soil."

- It is the business of this nation to put down other nations that would attempt to take peace from the world, which Satan is constantly promoting.
- It is the business of this nation, given by God, to protect the tiny state of Israel. Surrounded by a sea of Muslims, Israel is besieged from all sides. It is our responsibility to protect her against this hoard of hell.

If we as a nation discharge these responsibilities as we should, somehow God will see us through as it regards the constant problems that plague this nation and threaten to hurt, hinder, or even destroy her.

We are not wise in our thinking, Christians; we are not wise in our thinking, Americans, if we believe it is safe to let people who intend to do us harm cross our borders and live in our country.

The sensible thing to do is stop all immigration. That doesn't mean that we should stop showing Christian love to immigrants.

I know this issue has many believers struggling with verses such as Matthew 25:35: *"For I was hungry, and you gave Me meat: I was thirsty, and you gave Me drink: I was a stranger, and you took Me in."*

When this question came up on *Frances & Friends,* my husband called in to explain that this verse really pertains to Israel and the judgment of the nations in the coming kingdom age.

He said, "When the Lord will say that you have fed Me, He was talking about helping Israel. The world is obligated to help Israel, and God will bless those who do. This is what He's talking about in verse 25, not that Christians should take all of these people into their homes."

Consider the lawyer in Luke's gospel who "willing to justify himself" asked Jesus who his neighbor was. The Lord replied:

"But a certain Samaritan, as he journeyed, came where he was: and when he saw him, he had compassion on him, and went to him, and bound up his wounds, pouring in oil and wine, and set him on his own beast, and brought him to an inn, and took care of him" (Lk. 10:33-34).

Note that the Samaritan went to the man who had been attacked and robbed. He didn't bring him into his home. The Samaritan helped the injured man where he was and took him to a nearby inn and paid for his care.

America is a compassionate neighbor in the world and has poured $4.5 billion into the current immigration crisis. More U.S. dollars are being spent to bring refugees here, rather than help support the camps there.

Dr. Ben Carson recently visited a camp for Syrian refugees and asked what more America could do to help them. He said that they did not want to come to America. They would rather relocate within their own country, or at least in the nearby region.

"There's so many people who think the ideal for everybody is to come to America and be resettled here, but that is not the ideal for everybody," Carson said.

As Christians, of course we want to be compassionate and

show love to our fellow man, but our primary responsibility is to love and protect our families. Within the family unit, a husband's priority is to protect and provide for his family.

Likewise, the first and foremost duty of any U.S. president is to protect the citizens of the United States of America. Unfortunately, that is not the case with the current administration. As one political pundit put it, "We're on our own."

Still, we have people calling my program and arguing that Christians should take these Syrians — who have no desire to assimilate — into our country and into our homes. Donnie responded to those callers on the air:

"What if the next terrorist strike by one of those immigrants that we let in kills *your* grandchild, kills *your* son, kills *your* wife, or *your* husband," he said. "What's going to be your attitude then? It sounds harsh, it sounds mean, but it's not. We have to be vigilant to know who we let into our country because the lives — potential lives — of Americans are at stake, and it could be someone in *your* family."

Just two weeks after Donnie made that statement, a married couple living in California, loyal to Islam, planned and executed a mass shooting at the husband's San Bernardino workplace during a Christmas luncheon. They killed 14 people and injured 22. It was the worst terrorist attack on U.S. soil since 9/11.

We have to accept the harsh reality that Islamic terrorism is now growing up and living in the United States, and it will continue to grow if no one stops it.

I pray that America does not look back on these days

and say the same thing they said of the Holocaust: "Evil unchecked is the prelude to genocide."

As we've stated so many times, as the church goes, so goes the nation. I'm trying to wake up the church. I'm trying to wake up Christians. We have got to understand what evil is, and we've got to understand what Christian love is.

John Rosenstern put it well when he said, "As Christians, our love is sharing the gospel of Jesus Christ, who is love."

We demonstrate true Christian love through the preaching and teaching of the gospel. When He gave the Great Commission, the Lord did not say to open your borders to strangers. He did not say that to Solomon and He has not said that to us. His command is to go and preach — we go to them:

"Go ye into all the world, and preach the gospel to every creature" (Mk. 16:15).

Helping those in need with food, clothing, and shelter is good, but humanitarian efforts are a temporary fix; only the gospel of the Lord Jesus Christ has the power to save souls.

I can't think of a better testimony to this point than the one given by a precious lady named Jackie who called in to *Frances & Friends*.

She was born into a Muslim family in Turkey; the rest of her family is still Muslim. When she was 9 years old, her family moved to Berlin where she later became a born-again Christian. When Jackie converted to Christianity, her family disowned her because to them, she became a traitor.

Her own brother tried to kill her because in the Koran, people like her should be punished by death. When Jackie called in to the program, what she had to say just blessed me and everyone else on the panel. She said:

> The true Islam follows the teaching of Muhammad, the teaching of Koran. Everything you guys say are 100 percent true. I pray to God that every American gets a Koran and every person that never read the Koran that call themselves Muslim, please, please read the Koran and check the history. Then you will see everything my Sister Swaggart and her panel preach is the whole truth. We love Muslims. Jesus died for the Muslims. You know our war is not against people, our war is against the deceivers, the great deceiver — Satan himself. Pray for those men that call themselves ISIS.
>
> Jesus told us to love our enemies; He didn't say kill them. Muhammad says, 'Kill them wherever you find them.' Islam god says, 'Kill for me, then you come to heaven.' Our Jesus said, 'I died for you so you can come through Me to heaven.'
>
> My prayer is every Muslim receives Christ. And every person don't know Him, even in America. There are so many people call themselves Christians, but they're not Christians. We know that, because they're not living according to the Bible.

When I asked Jackie more about her brother trying to kill her, she added:

> Yes, ma'am, my brother threatened to kill me, tried to, yes, and he threatened me if I ever come to Turkey, if I ever share my Jesus, and I told him, 'If my Lord sends me there,

I'm coming. There's nothing that can stop me. Even if you kill me, every cell in my body will shout, 'Jesus, Jesus, Jesus' because He is life. There's no hope without Him; He is life. He is the cure for the world — not just for Americans, not just for Europe — He is for every human race if they want life and hope.

Because of Christianity, I have a personal experience with my God. He has revealed Himself to me personally. He has touched my life. He has changed my life. He changed my heart.

You know, Muslim is just a religion. God did not give us religion; He gave us a person, and His name is Jesus Christ.

This is a perfect picture of Christian love, both the receiving of it and the sharing of it. This precious woman heard the gospel and received the Lord as her personal Saviour.

This is what the preaching of the gospel does. Praise the Lord!

In her story, you can hear the boldness, the discernment, and the wisdom that the Lord has given her to deal with her family and to proclaim her testimony so that others have the opportunity to reach out to the Lord in faith. Most of all, you can hear the love she has for the Lord Jesus Christ.

Until we receive salvation, we are all spiritual refugees in need of the Saviour — the Lord Jesus Christ. That's why we work day and night to send the gospel out to all the nations around the world.

AND
SARAH
SAW

CHAPTER 4

COMMUNISM

COMMUNISM

KARL MARX WAS A German philosopher, sociologist, economic historian, journalist, and revolutionary socialist. He was heavily critical of the socio-economic form of society and taught that capitalism must be destroyed.

Marx tried to make capitalism the cause of all society's ills, but history has proven this notion wrong time and time again. Marx's theories about society, economics, and politics — collectively known as Marxism — hold that all societies progress through the dialectic of class struggle. Dialectic is a dialogue or method for resolving conflict between two or more people holding different points of view about a subject.

To Marx, this dialectic occurred between two main classes, the proletariat and the bourgeoisie. The proletariat is the labor or working class, the people who earn their livelihood by selling their labor power and being paid a wage or salary for their labor time. The bourgeoisie are those who earn their income not from labor as much as from the surplus value they appropriate from the workers who create wealth. And, according to Marx, the income of the capitalists is based on their exploitation of the workers (the proletariat). He thought that this conflict could not be abolished without replacing the system of capitalism itself.

You see, for Marx, democracy under capitalism is actually a bourgeois dictatorship.

THE COMMON MAN?

Now, at first glance, his theory makes Marx appear to be a man concerned for the "common man" and a friend to all, but let's dig a little deeper, first into Marx's psyche (and real beliefs), and secondly into the negative effects the system of socialism always has on a country.

Keep in mind that in order to change things, you must create a crisis, a reason for needing change. Marx used our human compassions for the poor to bring about his own political power, which was a power that would deny religious freedom in the end. The poor were not his cause but his vehicle to produce revolution.

Marx often quoted the phrase, "Religion is the opium of the people." We believers may concur with this statement in general, agreeing that yes, true Christianity is not a religion, but when Marx said it, he was referring to all religions, including true Christianity.

You have to keep in mind that his Marxist system, which was designed similarly to communism, would be used to oppress true Christianity, as is evident in the testimony of Brother Richard Wurmbrand, a believer who spent eight years in a communist prison for preaching the gospel and ideas contrary to communist doctrine.

Remember, socialism is something that sounds good on the surface but, in reality, is not. Its practical application does not hold up to its naive ideals. Yes, some employers and business owners take advantage of capitalism and exploit their workers, but we cannot forget that capitalism has a very important aspect. It allows for freedom!

If we allow for the loss of any freedom, eventually, we will lose all freedoms, even religious freedom! Carefully read this quote by Marx: "The abolition of religion as the illusory happiness of man is a requisite for their real happiness. The call to abandon their illusions about their conditions is a call to abandon a condition which requires illusion."

If we do not allow the opportunity for Americans (or people of any country) to make as much money as they desire, we eliminate the opportunity for all to make their desired amounts of income. God will take care of those who abuse the privilege.

"Behold, the hire of the laborers who have reaped down your fields, which is of you kept back by fraud, crieth: and the cries of them which have reaped are entered into the ears of the Lord of Sabaoth" (James 5:4).

WITHOUT GOD!

In his youth, Karl Marx professed to be a Christian. His father, a lawyer, was relatively prosperous and came from a

Jewish background, and his mother was a Dutch Jew from a prosperous business family. His maternal grandfather was a Jewish rabbi.

Prior to Karl's birth, his father converted from Judaism to the Protestant Christian denomination of Lutheranism. This is believed to be because he was barred from the practice of law due to being Jewish

So, the conversion could have been more for business reasons rather than actual spiritual ones. Nevertheless, Marx's first written work was called *The Union of the Faithful*, so there is evidence that Marx adhered to Christian beliefs early on.

However, for reasons unknown, he started to become very anti-religious. A new Marx began to emerge. He began to display a terrible hatred toward God. What exactly produced this hatred, no one seems to know.

He wrote the following line in his poem, "Invocation of One in Despair":

I shall build my throne high overhead.

In another poem he wrote:

Then I will be able to walk triumphantly, like a God, through the ruins of their kingdom.
Every word of mine is fire and action, my breast is equal to that of the Creator.

In his poem, "The Pale Maiden," he wrote:

Thus heaven I've forfeited, I know it full well.
My soul, once true to God, is chosen for hell.

Clearly, this man was very tormented. He went from blasphemous claims of considering himself equal to God to acknowledging he was going to a devil's hell.

THE DANCE OF DEATH

In reading Marx's poems, one quickly discovers not only that he hated God, but actually the gods of any religion.

In a little-known drama he composed, *Oulanem,* you see a very dark side of Karl developing — devil worship and the Black Mass. During a Black Mass, the Bible is burned and an orgy follows.

In a poem called "The Player," he pens these words:
The hellish vapors rise and fill the brain, till I go mad
    and my heart is utterly changed.
See this sword? The prince of darkness sold it to me.
For me beats the time and gives the signs.
Ever more boldly I play the dance of death.

Now, in the higher initiations of a satanist's cult, an "enchanted" sword, which ensures success, is sold to the candidate. He pays for it by signing a covenant — a blood oath. Yes, blood taken from his wrists, and he agrees that his soul will belong to Satan after death!

In his essay, *"The Eighteenth Brumaire,"* Marx quotes this: "Everything in existence is worth being destroyed."

These were the words of Mephistopheles in "Faust," and Marx loved these words. Stalin actually acted on these words and destroyed even his own family. In "Faust," the spirit that denies everything is called Satan.

In his poem, "Human Pride," Marx admits his aim is not to improve the world, reform, or revolutionize it, but simply to ruin it and to enjoy it being ruined.

He wrote, "With disdain I will throw my gauntlet full in the face of the world, and see the collapse of this pygmy giant whose fall will not stifle my ardor. Then will I wander godlike and victorious through the ruins of the world, and, giving my words an active force, I will feel equal to the Creator."

You see, in further, deeper study of Karl Marx, I found a man that had a deep hatred for God and for man as well. It was his desire to draw all of humanity into the abyss and to follow them laughing. And really, there is every evidence that Karl Marx was actually a Satanist. He is even buried in Highgate Cemetery in London. Highgate Cemetery is Britain's center of Satanism. Mysterious rites are held and celebrated at this tomb.

THE COMMUNIST MANIFESTO

In college Marx became involved with a group of radical thinkers known as the Young Hegelians, who gathered around Ludwig Feuerbach and Bruno Bauer. The Young Hegelians were critical of G. W. F. Hegel's metaphysical assumptions but still adopted his dialectic method in order to criticize established society, politics, and religion.

Marx befriended Bauer, and the two scandalized their class in Bonn by getting drunk, laughing in church, and galloping through the streets on donkeys. It was in Paris, on

Aug. 28, 1844, that Marx met German socialist, Friedrich Engels, and these two began a friendship that would last a lifetime.

On February 21, 1848, Marx and Engels's most famous work was published, which came to be known as, *The Communist Manifesto*. Marx and Engels both came from privileged families and both held a grudge against all religions.

"Running left-wing movements has always been the prerogative of spoiled rich kids ... The phoniness of the claim to be a movement of the working class was blatant from the beginning. When Engels was elected as a delegate to the Communist League in 1847, in his own words, 'a working man was proposed for appearances sake, but those who proposed him voted for me.'"

Marx also met Moses Hess, a man who played a most important role in his life, the man who led him to embrace the socialist ideal. No, Karl Marx did not love mankind. He was not prompted by concern for the poverty of his fellowman. He did not love them, but rather referred to them as nuts, asses, and rascals. He even described them using obscenities.

No, Marx's chief aim in life was the destruction of religion and to send mankind to hell. Marxists always appealed to the basest passions of men, such as stirring up envy toward the rich and encouraging violence. Marxists will exploit things such as racial differences or the so-called generation gap. They encourage an abolition of all morals, making everything permissible.

OCCULT SATANISM

Socialist and communist movements are, in reality, front organizations for occult Satanism. Karl Marx (and his satanic Marxism) is not a model for countries to follow, and any country that does follow this socialistic path will wind up broke with its people living in poverty, which is Satan's desire — to destroy God's creation.

The doctrine of socialism is seething with contradictions. Its theories are at constant odds with its practices. Indeed, no precise distinct socialism even exists. Instead, there is only a vague, rosy notion of something noble and good, of equality, of communal ownership, and of justice. It is believed that the advent of these things will bring instant utopia and a social order beyond reproach.

Yet, in any country that practices socialism or communism, you will not find any semblance of anything pertaining to a glorious future for its citizens. Look at China, Russia, and Europe. Look at the bloody experiments at the time of the reformation utopias of European thinkers, the intrigues of Marx and Engels, the radical communist measures of the Lenin period, or the heavy-handed methods of Stalin.

So, why is socialism being pushed down the throats of the American people today when it has always been a failure in any country of the world? It's plain and easy for anyone to see that socialism seeks to reduce human personality to its most primitive levels and to extinguish the highest and most God-like aspects of human individuality.

Actually, socialism has already proven to be a failed experiment here in the United States of America. The Pilgrims, the 104 people who arrived at Plymouth Rock on Dec. 21, 1620, were organized under a charter that imposed a seven year period of joint ownership. Thus, the day they arrived in the new world, all clothing, houses, land, crops, and cash were jointly owned.

So, no matter how hard a man might have worked, he had little hope of personal gain for his effort.

THE PILGRIMS

Thus, the Pilgrims started life in the New World with a system of common ownership forced on them by Plymouth Colony investors. That quasi-socialist arrangement proved to be disastrous. It had to be scrapped for one that gave these first Americans the right to keep the fruits of their labor and incentive to produce more. The communal arrangement also ill-fitted the Pilgrims for the demands of life on the edge of a cruel wilderness.

The Pilgrims buried 44 people within the first three months, and a total of 50 died within the first year. The ground proved to be unyielding, so Pilgrims gathered a small harvest and celebrated their first Thanksgiving with the Indians in the autumn of 1621. Another small harvest followed in 1622. Such a meager return came in part because the Pilgrims were unskilled at farming and because of the sandy New England soil.

However, it was the lack of any promise or return for their labors that caused even these God-fearing and devout settlers to fail to fully work the land. It also led to a social order at odds with the dictates of human nature, so there were dissensions and insubordination in unthrift and famine.

PRIVATE ENTERPRISE

In March of 1623, Governor Bradford allowed each man to plant corn for his own household and to trust themselves for that. So, every family was assigned a parcel of land, according to the proportion of their number. This proved to be very successful.

It made all hands very industrious, so that much more corn was planted than would have been by any other means anyone had devised. Suddenly, these heretofore mediocre farmers made their own capitalist "great leap forward."

Whereas 26 acres of corn, barley, and peas were planted in 1621, they planted nearly 60 acres the next year, and in 1623, they planted 184 acres. Governor Bradford reported that instead of famine, God gave them plenty, and things changed. And they gave thanks to God.

Under the new system of private enterprise, the Pilgrims grew in prosperity and were soon able to buy out the interest of their investors and obtain clear titles to their land.

Governor Bradford wrote this:

"The experience that was had in this common course and condition, tried sundry years and that amongst godly and sober men, may well evince the vanity of that conceit of Plato's and other ancients applauded by some of later times; that the taking away of property and bringing in community into a commonwealth would make them happy and flourishing; as if they were wiser than God."

Private enterprise is God-given and what this nation was founded on. Socialism, Marxism, and communism were all founded in satanism. Private industry is what America was established on, and it has resulted in the greatest nation ever produced on the face of the earth.

AND
SARAH
SAW

CHAPTER 5

CONDITIONED FOR
COMMUNISM

CONDITIONED FOR COMMUNISM

ON THURSDAY, JANUARY 10, 1963, Florida Congressman A. S. Herlong, Jr., stood on the floor of the U.S. House of Representatives and read a list of 45 "Current Communist Goals" — an excerpt, he said, from the book *The Naked Communist*.

All of these goals are listed at the end of this chapter, but I would like to comment on just a few of them:

Number 3: 'Develop the illusion that total disarmament by the United States would be a demonstration of moral strength.' [A simple comparison of the size and support of our armed forces now to what it was just 30 years ago will show how the U.S. military has been cut down again and again.]

Number 26: 'Present homosexuality, degeneracy, and promiscuity as "normal, natural, healthy."' [The president of the United States just appointed the first openly transgender man who dresses as a woman to be a recruitment director in the White House.]

Number 32: 'Eliminate prayer or any phase of religious

expression in the schools on the grounds that it violates the principle of "separation of church and state." This goal was met more than 50 years ago. In 1962 and 1963, the U.S. Supreme Court banned state-sponsored prayer in schools.]

I could go down the entire list of these communistic goals and show how each one has been accomplished — completely or in part — inside of one generation.

This infiltration of communistic ideals did not happen overnight. The change happened gradually — accelerating over the past 50 years as America shifted from her capitalist foundation to reach out for socialism and communitarianism, only to find herself completely conditioned for communism.

WHAT IS CAPITALISM, ANYWAY?

Webster's dictionary defines capitalism as a way of organizing an economy so that the things that are used to make and transport products — land, oil, factories, ships — are owned by individual people and companies rather than by the government.

We see capitalism taught throughout the Bible, beginning with the book of Genesis:

"And the LORD *God took the man, and put him into the garden of Eden to dress it and to keep it"* (Gen. 2:15).

God planted the garden, but He gave man the innovation, strength, and wisdom to work it. For Christians, this is capitalism in its truest form — believing in God's provision while doing the work at hand.

A WORD ABOUT WORK

In Proverbs, Chapter 14, Verse 23, we read, *"In all labor there is profit."* I believe that God expects all those who are able-bodied to work.

Having said that, I completely understand that some people — due to circumstances beyond their control or because of sickness or disability — simply cannot work. We sympathize with these precious people; they are the very ones our government absolutely should help and assist.

But there are millions of Americans out there who are capable of taking a job yet refuse to work.

Statistics show that of the 316 million people who live in the United States, 46 million receive food stamps. Think of that.

One news report claimed that the U.S. has more people dependent on food stamps than the total populations of Argentina, Columbia, Kenya, or Ukraine. The same report said, "Households on food stamps got an average benefit of $261.44 during the month, and total benefits for the month cost taxpayers $5,978,320,593."

So, basically, those who are working support those who either choose not to work or those who cannot work.

This dependency on government lines up with the communist agenda credited to Karl Marx.

His *Manifesto of the Communist Party* includes Frederick Engels'' "Draft of a Communist Confession of Faith," which is written in a question-and-answer format.

One question reads, "What will be your first measure once you have established democracy?"

The Marxist answer: "Guaranteeing the subsistence (amount of food, money needed to stay alive) of the proletariat (lowest social or economic class of a community)."

WHAT DOES GOD SAY ABOUT WORK?

When the Lord established the nation of Israel, He showed them how the nation was to be governed. He set their economy in motion with instruction on bartering, commerce, free enterprise, and trade. Provisions were also made for the poor:

"And when ye reap the harvest of your land, thou shalt not wholly reap the corners of thy field, neither shalt thou gather the gleanings of thy harvest. And thou shalt not glean thy vineyard, neither shalt thou gather every grape of thy vineyard; thou shalt leave them for the poor and stranger: I am the LORD your God" (Lev. 19:9-10).

Notice that the landowner did not gather the food and hand it over to the poor. No, his part was to leave some of the harvest — some of the work — for the poor to do.

We see this "law of gleanings" carried out in the Bible story of Boaz and Ruth:

"And when she was risen up to glean, Boaz commanded

his young men, saying, Let her glean even among the sheaves, and reproach her not: and let fall also some of the handfuls of purpose for her, and leave them, that she may glean them, and rebuke her not. So she gleaned in the field until evening, and beat out that she had gleaned: and it was about an ephah of barley" (Ruth 2:15-17).

Gleaning barley is hard, physical work, yet we see Ruth out there from morning until night doing what she needed to do to feed herself and her mother-in-law.

Nowhere in the Word of God will you find laziness rewarded in any shape, form, or fashion. Instead, you will find Scripture after Scripture condemning slack hands and slothful living:

"He becomes poor that deals with a slack hand: but the hand of the diligent makes rich" (Prov. 10:4).

"The hand of the diligent shall bear rule: but the slothful shall be under tribute" (Prov. 12:24).

"He also that is slothful in his work is brother to him that is a great waster" (Prov. 18:9).

"The desire of the slothful kills him; for his hands refuse to labor" (Prov. 21:25).

"But if any provide not for his own, and specially for those of his own house, he hath denied the faith, and is worse than an infidel" (I Tim. 5:8).

In America, we are guilty of rewarding laziness with our welfare programs. People who won't work (but laugh) go out and buy their alcohol and drugs with money for which we have worked very hard and paid in taxes to the federal government.

Then the federal government doles it out to people with no accountability for the money they receive. That's a sin.

God had no welfare program for Israel. He made no provision for people who were lazy. In Bible times, people who refused to work were looked down upon; they were outcasts of society, and they didn't exist for long.

God gives us the ability to work and expects us to work to provide, not only to help meet the needs of ourselves and our families, but also to have some left over to give to others.

In Ephesians 4:28 we read: *"Let him that stole steal no more: but rather let him labor, working with his hands the thing which is good, that he may have to give to him that needs."*

Christians are instructed to give to the Lord. The Bible shows Israel giving to build the tabernacle so the presence of God could dwell among them. Then we see the temple constructed, again so that the people could experience the presence of the Lord. Today we have the tithe, which helps support the place we worship the Lord and finances the propagation of the gospel of the Lord Jesus Christ.

America is a blessed nation because it has always been a Christian nation, a nation built on a strong work ethic — a capitalist nation. And it's the capitalist countries, not the communist ones, that are producing and have overflow.

I've been on the docks in foreign countries where goods are shipped in — food, water, and medical supplies — in response to something like a natural disaster, and all the food that's being brought in is coming from the United States of America. It's a patriotic feeling to see that huge ship and know it's from the United States of America. However, as patriotic as that may look or feel, goods and services are not this country's greatest export.

As you've probably heard my husband say many times, "As long as the gospel of Jesus Christ is America's greatest export, the jackbooted heels of foreign invaders will never walk on American soil."

Karl Marx may be the founder of communism, but God the Father is the founder of capitalism, and we must hold fast to God's way as outlined in His Word.

As Christians, we must continue to seek the face of the Lord and pray — especially heading into this most important election year — that America returns to her roots as a capitalist and a Christian nation.

45 COMMUNISTIC GOALS

Extension of Remarks of HON. A. S. HERLONG, JR., of Florida in the House of Representatives on Thursday, January 10, 1963. "Mr. HERLONG: Mr. Speaker, Mrs. Patricia Nordman of De Land, Florida, is an ardent and articulate opponent of communism, and until recently published the De Land Courier, which she dedicated to the purpose of alerting the public to the dangers of communism in America. At Mrs. Nordman's request, I include in the RECORD, under unanimous consent, the following "Current Communist Goals," which she identifies as an excerpt from *The Naked Communist*, by Cleon Skousen."

ACCOMPLISHED?

1. U.S. acceptance of coexistence as the only alternative to atomic war.

2. U.S. willingness to capitulate in preference to engaging in atomic war.

3. Develop the illusion that total disarmament by the United States would be a demonstration of moral strength.

4. Permit free trade between all nations regardless of Communist affiliation and regardless of whether or not items could be used for war.

5. Extension of long-term loans to Russia and Soviet satellites.

6. Provide American aid to all nations regardless of Communist domination.

7. Grant recognition of Red China. Admission of Red China to the U.N.

8. Set up East and West Germany as separate states in spite of Khrushchev's promise in 1955 to settle the German question by free elections under supervision of the U.N.

9. Prolong the conferences to ban atomic tests because the United States has agreed to suspend tests as long as negotiations are in progress.

10. Allow all Soviet satellites individual representation in the U.N.

11. Promote the U.N. as the only hope for mankind. If

its charter is rewritten, demand that it be set up 'as a one-world government' with its own Independent armed forces. (Some Communist leaders believe the world can be taken over as easily by the U.N. as by Moscow. Sometimes these two centers compete with each other as they are now doing in the Congo.)

12. Resist any attempt to outlaw the Communist Party.
13. Do away with all loyalty oaths.
14. Continue giving Russia access to the U.S. Patent Office.
15. Capture one or both of the political parties in the United States.
16. Use technical decisions of the courts to weaken basic American institutions by claiming their activities violate civil rights.
17. Get control of the schools. Use them as transmission belts for socialism and current Communist propaganda. Soften the curriculum. Get control of teachers' associations. Put the party line in textbooks.
18. Gain control of all student newspapers.
19. Use student riots to foment public protests against programs or organizations which are under Communist attack.
20. Infiltrate the press. Get control of book-review assignments, editorial writing, policymaking positions.
21. Gain control of key positions in radio, TV, and motion pictures.
22. Continue discrediting American culture by degrading

all forms of artistic expression. An American Communist cell was told to "eliminate all good sculpture from parks and buildings, substitute shapeless, awkward, and meaningless forms."

23. Control art critics and directors of art museums. "Our plan is to promote ugliness, repulsive, meaningless art."

24. Eliminate all laws governing obscenity by calling them "censorship" and a violation of free speech and free press.

25. Break down cultural standards of morality by promoting pornography and obscenity in books, magazines, motion pictures, radio, and TV.

26. Present homosexuality, degeneracy, and promiscuity, as "normal, natural, healthy."

27. Infiltrate the churches and replace revealed religion with "social" religion. Discredit the Bible and emphasize the need for intellectual maturity, which does not need a "religious crutch."

28. Eliminate prayer or any phase of religious expression in the schools on the ground that it violates the principle of "separation of church and state."

29. Discredit the America Constitution by calling it inadequate, old-fashioned, out of step with modern needs, a hindrance to cooperation between nations on a worldwide basis.

30. Discredit the American Founding Fathers. Present them as selfish aristocrats who had no concern for the "common man."

31. Belittle all forms of American culture and discourage the teaching of American history on the grounds that it was only a minor part of the "big picture." Give more emphasis to Russian history since the Communists took over.

32. Support any socialist movement to give centralized control over any part of the culture-education, social agencies, welfare programs, mental health clinics, etc.

33. Eliminate all laws or procedures which interfere with the operation of the Communist apparatus.

34. Eliminate the House Committee on Un-American Activities.

35. Discredit and eventually dismantle the FBI.

36. Infiltrate and gain control of more unions.

37. Infiltrate and gain control of big business.

38. Transfer some of the powers of arrest from the police to social agencies. Treat all behavioral problems as psychiatric, which no one but psychiatrists can understand or treat.

39. Dominate the psychiatric profession and use mental health laws as a means of gaining coercive control over those who oppose Communist goals.

40. Discredit the family as an institution. Encourage promiscuity and easy divorce.

41. Emphasize the need to raise children away from the negative influence of parents. Attribute prejudices, mental blocks, and retarding of children to suppressive influence of parents.

42. Create the impression that violence and insurrection are legitimate aspects of the American tradition; that students and special-interest groups should rise up and use united force to solve economic, political, or social problems.

43. Overthrow all colonial governments before native populations are ready for self-government.

44. Internationalize the Panama Canal.

45. Repeal the Connally Reservation so the United States cannot prevent the World Court from seizing jurisdiction over nations and individuals alike.

AND
SARAH
SAW

CHAPTER 6

CAPITALISM

CAPITALISM

ABRAHAM WAS CALLED OUT of the land of Ur to be the father of a new and separate race of people. Years later the Lord established the nation of Israel under the Mosaic covenant. At that time, God actually gave the nation detailed laws and regulations on how it was to be governed, how poverty was to be dealt with, how widows were to be helped, and how injustices were to be corrected.

Isn't that interesting? God even dealt with the economy. These matters were addressed almost exclusively within the context of the nation of Israel, showing little dealings concerning surrounding nations (this did change somewhat in the New Testament, which we will discuss later on).

THE LAW

In Leviticus 19:9-10, we read about the "law of gleanings." Under this law, the Israelites were to leave the corners of their fields and not glean or gather from them, but rather, they were to leave them for the poor to glean. This was to promote a general spirit of mercy to others who were suffering and in need.

This law even included the vineyards. The owners of the vineyards were not to gather all of the grapes in the vineyards. Some was to be left for the poor or the stranger that might wander into their lands. You see, the Lord provided several means to help the poor in Israel. There was also the concept of a "kinsman redeemer" (who was actually a type of Christ). A kinsman redeemer was a close relative designated to alleviate his relatives' troubles, including poverty.

Leviticus 25:25 explains that if a fellow countryman becomes so poor that he has to sell part of his property, then his nearest kinsman is to come and buy back the portion his relative had to sell. In the book of Ruth, we see a perfect example of how this worked.

In Deuteronomy 15:11, the Lord tells Israel: *"The poor shall never cease out of* (to be in) *the land: therefore I command you, saying, You shall open your hand wide* (freely open) *unto your brother, to your poor, and to your needy, in your land."*

In Isaiah 10:1-2, the Lord tells His people: *"Woe unto them who decree unrighteous decrees* (those who enact evil statutes), *and who write grievousness which they have prescribed* (to those who constantly record unjust decisions); *to turn aside the needy from judgment* (so as to deprive the needy of justice), *and to take away the right from the poor of My people* (rob the poor of their rights), *that widows may be their prey* (so that widows may be their spoil), *and that they may rob the fatherless* (plunder the orphans)."

The poor, needy, and destitute were cared for, but notice, it was not an entitlement program or a system that allowed the lazy to avoid working that God instituted. Rather, it was a system that taught mercy and love. It was simply designed to help those who were unable to help themselves. Laziness was not rewarded.

GOD'S WAY

Consider what the Scriptures have to say on this subject:

Proverbs 10:4: *'He becomes poor who deals with a slack hand: but the hand of the diligent makes rich.'*

Proverbs 10:5: *'He who gathers in summer is a wise son: but he who sleeps in harvest is a son that causes shame.'*

Proverbs 12:24: *'The hand of the diligent shall bear rule: but the slothful shall be under tribute.'*

Proverbs 14:23: *'In all labor there is profit: but the talk of the lips tendeth only to penury.'*

Proverbs 18:9: *'He also who is slothful in his work is brother to him that is a great waster.'*

Proverbs 19:15: *'Slothfulness casts into a deep sleep; and an idle soul shall suffer hunger.'*

Proverbs 20:4: *'The sluggard will not plow by reason of the cold; therefore shall he beg in harvest, and have nothing.'*

Proverbs 21:25: *'The desire of the slothful kills him; for his hands refuse to labor.'*

Proverbs 23:21: *'For the drunkard and the glutton shall come to poverty: and drowsiness shall clothe a man with rags.'*

Ecclesiastes 10:18: *'By much slothfulness the building decays; and through idleness of the hands the house drop-peth through.'*

II Thessalonians 3:10-11: *'For even when we were with you, this we commanded you, that if any would not work, nei-ther should he eat. For we hear that there are some who walk among you disorderly, working not at all, but are busybodies.'*

This last verse is particularly interesting because it points out that God puts refusal to work in the category of disorder. Remember the true blessings of God come as we walk in His will.

If we are out of order, it will limit what God can do for us. Welfare programs were not put in place to benefit the poor, and food stamps were not given away in Israel, but rather, grain was left in the field for the poor to glean, grapes were left in the vineyards, and a kinsman redeemer helped the orphaned and widowed. What I want the reader to under-stand is that each person had to provide for himself and his family to the best of his ability.

COMMERCE

There was also commerce in Israel, as the following Scrip-tures indicate:

I Kings 10:28-29: *"And Solomon had horses brought out of Egypt, and linen yarn: the king's merchants received the linen yarn at a price. And a chariot came up and went out of Egypt for six hundred shekels of silver, and an horse for an hundred and fifty: and so for all the kings of the Hittites, and for the kings of Syria, did they bring them out by their means."*

II Chronicles 9:21: *"For the king's ships went to Tarshish with the servants of Huram: every three years once came the ships of Tarshish bringing gold, and silver, ivory, and apes, and peacocks."*

Proverbs 31:14-18: *"She is like the merchants' ships; she brings her food from afar. She rises also while it is yet night, and gives meat to her household, and a portion to her maidens. She considers a field, and buys it: with the fruit of her hands she plants a vineyard. She girds her loins with strength, and strengthens her arms. She perceiveth that her merchandise is good: her candle goes not out by night."*

Proverbs 11:26: *"He who withholds corn, the people shall curse him: but blessing shall be upon the head of him who sells it."* Isaiah 23:3: *"And by great waters the seed of Sihor, the harvest of the river, is her revenue; and she is a mart of nations."*

Mark 11:15-17: *"And they come to Jerusalem: and Jesus went into the temple, and began to cast out them who sold and bought in the temple, and overthrew the tables of* the moneychangers, and the seats of them who sold doves; and would not suffer that any man should carry any vessel through the temple. And He taught, saying unto them, Is it not written, My house shall be called of all nations the house of prayer? but you have made it a den of thieves."

TRADE

The Bible also has much to say on the subject of trade:

Acts 19:23-28:
'And the same time there arose no small stir about that way. For a certain man named Demetrius, a silversmith, who made silver shrines for Diana, brought no small gain unto the craftsmen; whom he called together with the workmen of like occupation, and said, Sirs, you know that by this craft we have our wealth. Moreover you see and hear, that not alone at Ephesus, but almost throughout all Asia, this Paul has persuaded and turned away much people, saying that they be no gods, which are made with hands: so that not only this our craft is in danger to be set at nought; but also that the temple of the great goddess Diana should be despised, and her magnificence should be destroyed, whom all Asia and the world worships. And when they heard these sayings, they were full of wrath, and cried out, saying, Great is Diana of the Ephesians.'

Revelation 18:11-13:

> *'And the merchants of the earth shall weep and mourn over her; for no man buys their merchandise any more: the merchandise of gold, and silver, and precious stones, and of pearls, and fine linen, and purple, and silk, and scarlet, and all thyine wood, and all manner vessels of ivory, and all manner vessels of most precious wood, and of brass, and iron, and marble, and cinnamon, and odours, and ointments, and frankincense, and wine, and oil, and fine flour, and wheat, and beasts, and sheep, and horses, and chariots, and slaves, and souls of men.'*

I Kings 10:28-29: *"And Solomon had horses brought out of Egypt, and linen yarn: the king's merchants received the linen yarn at a price. And a chariot came up and went out of Egypt for six hundred shekels of silver, and an horse for an hundred and fifty: and so for all the kings of the Hittites, and for the kings of Syria, did they bring them out by their means."*

Ezekiel 27:12: *"Tarshish was your merchant by reason of the multitude of all kind of riches; with silver, iron, tin, and lead, they traded in your fairs."*

ECONOMY

Bartering is also mentioned in the Word of God:

Genesis 47:15-17:

> *'And when money failed in the land of Egypt, and in the land of Canaan, all the Egyptians came unto*

Joseph, and said, Give us bread: for why should
we die in your presence? for the money fails. And
Joseph said, Give your cattle; and I will give you for
your cattle, if money fail. And they brought their
cattle unto Joseph: and Joseph gave them bread in
exchange for horses, and for the flocks, and for the
cattle of the herds, and for the asses: and he fed
them with bread for all their cattle for that year.'

I Kings 5:10-11: "So Hiram gave Solomon cedar trees
and fir trees according to all his desire. And Solomon gave
Hiram twenty thousand measures of wheat for food to his
household, and twenty measures of pure oil: thus gave Solomon
to Hiram year by year."

The Bible also speaks of payment:

Genesis 14:22-24: "And Abram said to the king of
Sodom, I have lift up my hand unto the LORD, the Most
High God, the possessor of heaven and earth, That I will
not take from a thread even to a shoelatchet, and that I will
not take any thing that is yours, lest you should say, I have
made Abram rich: Save only that which the young men
have eaten, and the portion of the men who went with me,
Aner, Eshcol, and Mamre; let them take their portion."

Ezra 3:7: "They gave money also unto the masons, and
to the carpenters; and meat, and drink, and oil, unto them
of Zidon, and to them of Tyre, to bring cedar trees from
Lebanon to the sea of Joppa, according to the grant that
they had of Cyrus king of Persia."

Romans 4:4: *"Now to him who works is the reward not reckoned of grace, but of debt."*

Ephesians 1:14: *"Which is the earnest of our inheritance until the redemption of the purchased possession, unto the praise of His glory."*

WORK AND LABOR

Work and labor are actually mentioned in many Scriptures.

Genesis 2:15: *"And the LORD God took the man, and put him into the garden of Eden to dress it and to keep it."*

Genesis 3:17-19:

> *'And unto Adam He said, Because you have hearkened unto the voice of thy wife, and have eaten of the tree, of which I commanded you, saying, You shall not eat of it: cursed is the ground for your sake; in sorrow shall you eat of it all the days of your life; Thorns also and thistles shall it bring forth to you; and you shall eat the herb of the field; In the sweat of your face shall you eat bread, till you return unto the ground; for out of it were you taken: for dust you art, and unto dust shall you return.'*

Jeremiah 22:13: *"Woe unto him who builds his house by unrighteousness, and his chambers by wrong; that uses his neighbour's service without wages, and gives him not for his work."*

Leviticus 19:13: *"You shall not defraud thy neighbour, neither rob him: the wages of him who is hired shall not abide with you all night until the morning."*

Deuteronomy 24:14: *"You shall not oppress an hired servant who is poor and needy, whether he be of your brethren, or of your strangers who are in your land within your gates."*

Exodus 20:9: *"Six days shall you labour, and do all your work."*

Psalms 104:23: *"Man goes forth unto his work and to his labour until the evening."*

FREE ENTERPRISE

I could give many more Scriptures, but for lack of space, I will mention only a few more to show what the Bible teaches about laborers being worthy of their hire.

Luke 10:7: *"And in the same house remain, eating and drinking such things as they give: for the laborer is worthy of his hire. Go not from house to house."*

I Timothy 5:18: *"For the Scripture says, You shall not muzzle the ox that treads out the corn. And, The labourer is worthy of his reward."*

In the Old Testament, we see that ownership of land was taught. In II Samuel 24:18-24, we see David going to Araunah the Jebusite to purchase a threshingfloor to build an altar unto the Lord. Araunah tells David he will give it to him, along with the oxen, the wood, and the threshing instruments. But, in Verse 24, king David replies, *"No; but I will surely buy it of thee at a price."*

In the Old Testament, a person's wealth was determined by how much land and by how many sheep, oxen, goats, camels, etc. he had. God gave land to His nation, and they were to take and divide it among the tribes of Israel. Along with laws and a system of government, every man and woman was given their inherited land, land to work, buy, sell, farm and grow their crops, and feed their cattle. But, of course, first and foremost was their worship of God.

Today this free enterprise is called capitalism. Our forefathers took great pains to make sure our nation was founded upon economic freedoms, as well as other freedoms, for every man, woman, and child.

The United States was established upon liberating, constitutional principles and steeped in free-market capitalism. It is a proud heritage, and because of the opportunities that it offered, America was populated by an industrious people, individuals who labored diligently to build the most historically powerful nation on earth!

Unfortunately today, many citizens are failing to understand its value. It used to be a nation whose people were people of worth and dignity, a nation of which the people were embedded with a work ethic that excelled that of any other nation. It was a nation in which it was considered immoral and shameful to accept unearned handouts or to live off the sweat of another man's brow.

However, we have been infested by a bunch of socialist

and communist crusaders (most of whom have never worked an honest day's work in their lives), who promote the Communist Manifesto over our U.S. Constitution and harbor disdain of the free-market system, to which they actually owe their lofty existence and high stations.

God help us come back to our foundations or this country will not remain the same.

AND SARAH SAW

TRUE TO CULTURE
OR TO CHRIST?

TRUE TO CULTURE OR TO CHRIST?

"**IN AMERICA, THE CHURCH** is still the most segregated major institution in America. At 11:00 on Sunday morning when we stand and sing and Christ has no east or west, we stand at the most segregated hour in this nation."

— Martin Luther King, Jr.,
speaking at Western Michigan University, 1963

In the summer of 2008, after receiving several emails regarding a discussion held over SonLife Radio on *Frances & Friends*, we felt we needed to further address this issue of segregation. This is one letter that was written on the subject:

First and foremost I thank God for your boldness by which you preach and teach Jesus Christ and the Cross, Him crucified for our salvation. My my husband and I pray for you daily. We tuned in to your program this evening when discussion was taking place regarding politics and primarily Mr. Obama. We are less concerned about the election and more concerned about race relations in this country. It seems like this 'unexpected' popularity of Obama has brought out so many fears. I was shocked to hear your comment that he supports 'black supremacy' in this country. What does that mean? I already wear the color and know that 'race does matter' in America. And many have forgotten that this country was built with 300 years of free slave labor. Immigrants got paid for their contributions. Mrs. Swaggart, I accept that you have human limitations imposed by the color of your skin. Yes, in America race does matter, as shown on Sunday mornings. Since the Lord is coming back for a church without spot or wrinkle, race is still one area that has to be smoothed out. I am, and always have been an Independent (voted twice for Bush) and am not saying that I even know who I will vote for. Obama is an individual running for president. How did he end up being a threat to the white race? He's either a threat to America which includes us all or he isn't. God has always used the church (His people) to move America. My prayer is that His church will once again learn to listen to His voice. We love you all with the love of the Lord.

DOCTRINAL

First of all, please allow me to elaborate on the discussion held during that radio program. It was not of a political nature, but rather of a doctrinal nature. We were adamantly disagreeing with the doctrine held by Senator Obama's pastor, Rev. Jeremiah Wright of Trinity United Church of Christ. His church espouses this: "We are an African people, and remain 'true to our native land,' the mother continent, the cradle of civilization. God has superintended our pilgrimage through the days of slavery, the days of segregation, and the long night of racism. It is God who gives us the strength and courage to continuously address injustice as a people, and as a congregation. We constantly affirm our trust in God through cultural expression of a black worship service and ministries which address the black community."

CULTURE

When the believer is saved, he is saved out of his culture, not in it. If this was not true, then the Jewish followers of Christ discussed in the Bible would have been allowed to hold on to their traditions. Their customs had been in place longer than any other civilization in the world.

But the Jewish Christians were not concerned with their old roots. They knew that when Christ, the Messiah, came, they were to forsake all of their old traditions and follow Him. Born-again believers, no matter what background they come from, have been given new roots, hallelujah! Now that is something worth shouting from every rooftop, something truly worth being loyal to!

As a matter of fact, the Bible warns us against following the traditions of men:

"As you have therefore received Christ Jesus the Lord, so walk you in him: Rooted and built up in Him, and established in the faith, as you have been taught, abounding therein with thanksgiving. Beware lest any man spoil you

through philosophy and vain deceit, after the tradition of men, after the rudiments of the world, and not after Christ" (Col. 2:6-8).

This is true for every cultural background. When the Native American accepts Christ, he should forsake all forms of the worship of other gods — the powwows, totem poles, dances, medicine men, etc. I could even say that about myself. I am of Scottish and Irish descent, but I do not hold to the Celtic traditions of my ancestors or their religion. Neither do I hold to the traditions of my Native American heritage.

"Therefore if any man be in Christ, he is a new creature: old things are passed away; behold, all things are become new" (II Cor. 5:17).

While we are all very much aware of our past culture and history, we cannot continue to live in the past. It is important to recognize that inevitably all of the ethnic behaviors of men come back to some form of religious belief — and a belief that does not tell us we are justified by faith alone.

Christians live exclusively by faith in the finished work of Calvary because we have come to realize that it is by His work alone that man may prosper. This is, in essence, the new "culture" of Christ. And it explains why so many today have trouble coming out of their old traditions. It directly insults man's pride of life. Man cannot save himself, provide for himself, or better himself in any way, but yet, this is exactly what the cultures of man were designed to do — prosper the society.

The Cross is truly a slap in the face to every way of mankind.

However, we should realize that it is a rebuke to our selfishness and self-dependence that keeps us out of fellowship with God, so the insult actually comes from love. God wants us to be able to fellowship with Him, but such can only come through a complete death to self at the foot of Calvary.

FREEDOM OF RELIGION

The very reason for the Reformation in the 1500s was because of the traditions of men that had gone on for so long. If Martin Luther, along with many other of the great reformers at the time, had not decided to step out and come away from the established church and traditions of that day, we would still be living in a society ruled and controlled by a government based upon false religion. And if that had happened, as horrible as the initial time of Africans coming to this country was, millions of African-Americans would have simply remained African and not known the freedom and prosperity that America has had to offer at all.

So, for any church leader to get up and tell the people that they are going to be "true to our native land, the mother continent, or the cradle of civilization," they are remaining true to a culture and not to Christ. You simply cannot have both.

It is because of Christ that America believes in freedom of religion, and it is because of Christ that any of us have been given freedom from sin. The native land of Africa did not provide freedom, safety, or salvation for African-Americans, nor did their African ancestors. In fact, it was many of their own people — other Africans — who sold them into slavery in the first place. So, why would such a history deserve the African-American's loyalty today?

On the note of racism, please allow me to preface my comments by saying the following: If you were to walk into Family Worship Center on any given day of the week, you will see what the body of Christ truly is. We have a congregation of Caucasian, African American, Hispanic, Native American, and any number of other nationalities. Any and all races are welcomed, and the wonderful thing is that no matter what, as the Spirit of God moves, everyone enters in to the presence of the Lord and worships. The Spirit of God knows no cultural boundaries.

SAVED OR UNSAVED

Having said that, Rev. Wright very prominently says on his website that the motto of their church is, "We are a congregation which is unashamedly black and unapologetically Christian ... Our roots in the black religious experience and tradition are deep, lasting and permanent."

As well, he unashamedly holds to the ideals promoted within the Black Power Movement. What if a white pastor got up and said we are "unashamedly white and unapologetically Christian?" Actually, we do have those groups, and such white supremacy groups are evil.

Are they the picture of Christianity? Absolutely not!

There is only one dividing line in the eyes of God — saved

or unsaved. Anyone who belittles this or tries to create more divisions is doing injustice to Christ and His Cross.

The other problem we had with this pastor is his support of Louis Farrakhan, who is a self-proclaimed Muslim, and whose teachings are very much pulling people away from the body of Christ as a whole.

How can any preacher of the gospel support such a religious leader? To be blunt, they cannot. It doesn't matter how much a man seemingly fights for civil rights or racial equality if he does not stand for Christ.

Is your pride as a race really more important than the truth of the gospel? Are you willing to team up with a man who serves Allah just to have one more black man in Congress? Think about it. Whom do you serve?

When we put aside the racial issue and look at the spiritual issue, we simply have to take a stand against what is being taught from a spiritual perspective — whether it is being taught by a black man or a white man. If you will fight for Christ, He will fight for you! He will prosper you in His way and in His time if you put your loyalties to Him first.

CHRIST SUPREMACY

We should not wish for any type of racial supremacy in this nation at all. We should pray for Christ's supremacy. If any ethnic group becomes driven by the desire to be supreme, it is no longer classified as Christianity. It is racism. Webster's dictionary defines racism as, "a belief that race is the primary determinant of human traits and capacities and that racial differences produce an inherent superiority of a particular race."

So, whether it is a Hispanic, African-American, Caucasian, Asian, or any other who promotes an agenda for the sole sake of benefiting his personal race, he is, by default, guilty of racism himself.

I hope in America today we would look for leaders who first and foremost are Christian, not in name only, but evidenced in the life they live and the doctrine they hold to (Lk. 21:8).

I think you know by now, through listening to our program, that we have dealt with people across a broad spectrum of religious beliefs. It is amazing to me that no one has accused us of racial bias when we have dealt with *The Purpose Driven Life*, Government of 12, or even the religious background of our current president. We will not hold back from discussing the doctrine of any false religion or teaching, regardless of the color of the man's skin that is purporting it.

RACIAL LINES

The truth is that the Christian church has been divided across racial lines. In the political arena, we have the majority of black Christians voting for the Democratic Party because they are led to believe Democrats more readily promote minority equality.

On the other side, we have the majority of white Christians

voting for the Republican Party because they believe this is the party that stands for Christian morals.

Can't we as Christians see that this is really just a trick of the Devil to divide and conquer the body of Christ? Why didn't the church recognize the danger of America's two-party politics a long time ago?

Jesus clearly stated: *"Every kingdom divided against itself is brought to desolation; and every city or house divided against itself shall not stand"* (Mat. 12:25).

JESUS ALONE DESERVES YOUR LOYALTY

There is an excellent article on the *News With Views* website that I recommend everyone should read. It was written by Dave Daubenmire and entitled, "What Color Is Your Christianity?"

In this article Mr. Daubenmire states:

Black Christians are voting for candidates who won't stop the killing of unborn black babies ... 'White churches,' for the most part have been oblivious to the needs of their black brothers and sisters in Christ ... We have turned the duties of the church over to the god-of-government and we wonder why our black brothers look to elected officials for salvation.

Daubenmire continues:

'White Christians' pray to their 'white God' for more stuff, while 'black Christians' pray to their 'black God' for justice and equality ... Tragically, most blacks have been taught to be more loyal to the Democrats than they are to their Lord and how about you, my white Christian brother? Did Jeremiah Wright's comments make you angry or sad? Are you voting Republican so you can beat the Democrats when you should be voting for Jesus so he can destroy the works of Satan? We have become convinced that Party allegiance trumps allegiance to Christ. The Devil runs both Parties. A vote for either is a vote for Slewfoot's agenda. What kind of nation would this be if 90 percent of the Christians voted for the same values? ... Blacks and whites serve the same Jesus. We just don't know that we do.

God, forgive us all for being so blind!

The apostle Paul said: *"Be ye followers of me, even as I also am of Christ"* (I Cor. 11:1).

All true believers must begin disregarding cultural backgrounds and start choosing leaders, both political and spiritual, whose actions are directed by Christ rather than his race. Do not allow race become an idol. It is only Jesus who deserves your loyalty.

AND SARAH SAW

CHAPTER 8

COMMON CORE: EDUCATION OR INDOCTRINATION?

COMMON CORE: EDUCATION OR INDOCTRINATION?

IN THE SPRING OF 1989, Angela Buller stood up at her high school graduation and gave her valedictory speech. The remarks she gave nearly 30 years ago, which I will share in part below, are important now because of the school she attended.

Angela attended the Robert Muller School, named after Dr. Robert Muller, who served for 40 years as assistant secretary-general for the United Nations. There, he was known as the "prophet of hope" of the United Nations. His website biography claims that Muller was a "deeply spiritual" person; others credit his religious convictions to his increased representation of religions in the UN, especially the New Age Movement.

His website also names his "spiritual master" — UN Secretary General U Thant — a former school headmaster, who often told Muller, "Robert, there will be no peace on earth if there is not a new education."

Muller created the World Core Curriculum for which he received the UN Educational Scientific and Cultural Organization Peace Education Prize and became known as the "father of global education." The content of his curriculum is summarized in four pillars: Our planetary home and place in the universe; humanity; our place in time; and the miracle of individual life (this includes spiritual exercises of interiority, meditation, and prayer and communion with the universe and eternity *or* God). Today, there are 29 of Muller's schools worldwide.

Angela Buller was the first graduate and first valedictorian from his school. At her graduation ceremony, instead of inspiring her fellow students about their futures, Angela used her speech to praise the school's curriculum:

> We started out searching for a global curriculum, but we didn't have one until the World Core Curriculum was implemented. This curriculum has broadened the scope of the learning experience so that my understanding of relationships is much more comprehensive than traditional education allows. I feel I know something about the Cosmos, the planetary organism, its various kingdoms, its people and their cultures, and how all that relates to me. I feel I have some perspective on how I fit into it all — the universe, the planet, and its ecology and cultures.
>
> As I have become older, I have begun to grasp how deeply I have been affected by the broad scope of the curriculum — on subtle levels of consciousness. I have not analyzed how the World Core Curriculum is put together, but I have realized the results — my understanding of the relationships which I mentioned is real and will always have an affect on my attitudes to life.

This is what Muller's curriculum produced: a student who strongly supported a new age curriculum, even though she didn't know how it came about. Yet, its effects shaped her attitude throughout life.

If the tenets and student impact of the World Core Curriculum sound familiar, it's because the standards now set in most U.S. public schools have their roots in World Core. Today it's called Common Core.

The name has changed, but the indoctrination goals of Common Core echo Muller's objectives to "steer our children towards global citizenship, earth-centered beliefs, socialist values and collective mindset which is becoming a requirement for the 21st century workforce."

As a guest panelist on *Frances & Friends,* Kathryn Goppelt, an educator with 30 years of teaching experience and an advocate for parents and teachers against Common Core, confirmed Muller's involvement.

"Common Core ... started in 1984; it was called World Core curriculum," she said. "The goal of Common Core is to bring the world into one philosophical, religious, and academic oneness or sameness."

WHAT IS COMMON CORE?

The official website for the Common Core State Standards answers the question this way:

"State education chiefs and governors in 48 states came together to develop the Common Core, a set of clear college- and career-ready standards for kindergarten through 12th grade in English language arts/literacy and mathematics. Today, 42 states and the District of Columbia have voluntarily adopted and are working to implement the standards, which are designed to ensure that students graduating from high school are prepared to take credit bearing introductory courses in two- or four-year college programs or enter the workforce."

Emmett McGroarty, the director of education at the American Principles Project and co-author of the book, *Controlling Education from the Top: Why Common Core is Bad for America*, was also a guest on *Frances & Friends*. He said that governors committed their states to Common Core based on its promise: that standards would be internationally benchmarked, evidence-based, and rigorous.

"They committed their states before Common Core had been developed. A year and a half later, the final product of the Common Core came out and it failed to meet those slogans, those goals," he said. "But at that point, all these governors and school boards had painted themselves into the corner, and I think they felt it was too damaging to their political careers to get out. What they failed to consider is how damaging it would be to the children and to our Constitution."

Dr. Sandra Stotsky, English professor emeritus of the University of Arkansas and former Senior Associate Commissioner of the Massachusetts Department of Education, was on the Common Core validation committee from 2009-2010.

Stotsky said the decision to adopt Common Core standards was made by, in most cases, state boards of education:

> They are the responsible group. The groups that were bypassed in this very narrow decision-making kind of process were, first of all, parents; second of all, teachers; third of all, state legislators; and fourth, local school boards and committees all over the country. They knew essentially nothing about what their state boards of education were committing themselves to and these state boards of education did not ask, in any case that I have asked about, they have not shown that they, in any way, tried to find out what the strings were that were attached to Common Core, or what Common Core standards were actually all about.

HUMAN CAPITAL

Education historian and New York University research professor Diane Ravitch said that advocates of Common Core believed that the standards would "automatically guarantee equity."

In a speech to the Modern Language Association, Ravitch said: "Some spoke of the Common Core as a civil rights issue. They emphasized that the Common Core standards would be far more rigorous than most state standards and they predicted that students would improve their academic performance in response to raising the bar."

When did public education become a civil rights issue? Let's call it what it is: Common Core is a bold push into socialism — a transitional phase between capitalism and communism — that is devastating the American educational system.

McGroarty explains this drastic swing that views the individual radically differently than our Founding Fathers did:

> Our founders were of the view that each individual was the ultimate earthly sovereign and that people can direct their own lives, and raise their own children, make their decisions and chart their own course in life. And traditional education in America supported that idea — supported the development of a child into an adult who could pursue the truth — and especially through the study of literature, could hone their analytical thinking skills and their abilities to empathize with others. And that's kind of the traditional view of education in America.
>
> [Common Core] kind of turns that on it's head and looks at the individual as human capital who has to be educated in order to meet the needs of corporatism — big corporations that want workers, not really the exact number of workers they need, but an abundance of workers — more than they need. And it doesn't further the goals of a country that is premised on citizen-directed government; it doesn't further the goals of entrepreneurship; it doesn't further the goals of capitalism.

Jane Robbins, an attorney and senior fellow with the American Principles Project, agreed. In her five-part video series, *Stop The Common Core*, Robbins said:

It's a progressive school-to-work dream to think that government finally will have all the tools in place to plan for future labor markets. Progressives, or socialists, as they have been historically known, have long sought to create a managed economy.... Through our schools, the next generation will be conditioned to accept that government has the right to direct them to serve the economic priorities of the nation, or any other priorities the government deems best. In other words, government will no longer be their servant, but will become their master, and the individual will exist to serve the purposes of society.

The standardization goals of Common Core for our public schools are part of a global agenda that is hurting our children now. Parents write to me and ask, "What is happening in my child's classroom?" After attending a forum on Common Core, one parent emailed me and said he was nearly brought to tears thinking about the future of his children. "They will never know the America I know," he said. That just breaks my heart.

UNPREPARED

The Common Core State Initiative targets how and what children learn. Since testing is the way these so-called rigorous new standards are measured and how teachers are evaluated, then the standardized tests drive the curriculum — currently English language arts and math. So, let's take a look at what's happening to those subjects.

As previously mentioned, Stotsky was on the Common Core validation committee from 2009 to 2010. Also on that committee was Dr. James Milgram, a professor of mathematics at Stanford University who is an internationally-known mathematician.

Both Stotsky and Milgram were frustrated because they repeatedly asked for but never received the list of other countries benchmarked with the U.S. in the subjects of math and English.

In her YouTube video, "Common Core National Education Standards," Stotsky explained why she refused to validate Common Core.

"We could not find out what countries we were benchmarked with in mathematics or English language arts, and [Milgram] could tell, from the topics that were mentioned in the mathematics standards, by grade 8, U.S. students would be about two years behind their peers in high-achieving countries. It's less easy to tell in the English language arts. I would certainly agree, in general, that Common Core's standards were not to be preparing American students for authentic college work in a subject."

Stotsky went on to explain in her video how Common Core has reduced the number of literary texts, "particularly those written before the 1970s," because the mandate is for at least 50 percent *informational* reading and writing.

"That division of reading instruction also diminishes the ability of students to develop critical thinking skills, which is another false claim of the Common Core standard," Stotsky said. "It will not improve critical thinking skills; it will reduce the ability to develop critical thinking skills because students will develop how to read between the lines of the complex literary text they once were taught how to read."

Dr. Terrence Moore, a history professor at Hillsdale College, is also concerned about the reading content now replacing historic documents and classic literature under Common Core.

On February 20, 2014, he joined our panel on *Frances & Friends* along with Stotsky, Milgram, Robbins, and McGroarty to share his concerns.

"The Common Core, at least as far as the English standards are concerned, and as later will be the case for the history standards, which are right around the corner, is the attempt to take away the great stories of the American people and replace them with the stories that fit the progressive liberal narrative of the world. As such, the architects of the Common Core are nothing less than story killers. They are deliberately killing the greatest stories of the greatest nation in history."

Moore said that Common Core is "anti-family and anti-religious" and pointed out that articles about government agenda items on healthcare and the environment are replacing classic literature, including any references to the Bible, historical sermons, or even texts inspired by religious tradition.

Fictional classics that did survive the standards have been, in some cases, reduced to excerpts. Pieces of books like *To Kill A Mockingbird* are now read alongside articles such as

"Shaking the Heavens in Ferguson, Missouri," published in the *New York Times.*

The Common Core math standards are even more disturbing. Today's child, under Common Core, can say 1+1=3, and his answer will not be counted wrong as long as he can show how he arrived at his incorrect answer. That's frightening.

In a discussion about America's educational ranking in the world — some say 5th, 6th or 7th — I asked my panel of distinguished educators if they thought Common Core was purposely dumbing down American students. Milgram said yes and offered the following:

> This is a long term problem, of course, and it's not 5th, 6th or 7th — it's 21st, 22nd, 23rd and it's actually probably lower than that in mathematics. Then the question becomes, does Common Core show any interest or potential to improve that? And oddly enough, the answer is absolutely not.

What happens is that we've gone back to another of these programs that we know absolutely failed because the evidence is overwhelming, and that's the new math in the 1960s. And that's what they were doing in the new math in the 1960s and, of course, there was a huge reaction against that in the 1970s, and the new math disappeared. But now we're back, with a known failed program, and the idea that you don't learn the basic algorithms, you learn all the things around them, and you produce your own individual algorithms for doing calculations, which may or may not be correct. All of this is back and it's what the kids are dealing with now, and it's not what mathematics is all about.

COMMUNIST CORE

Still, the creators and proponents of Common Core insist that these standards will make U.S. students competitive in the global workplace. But is this the reality or the rhetoric?

Lily Tang Williams is one of many parents standing up against these standards. Read carefully her testimony before the board of education in her state of Colorado:

I am Chinese immigrant. I do not buy into Common Core. I am here to oppose it strongly because I can tell you Common Core, in my eyes, is as same as Communist Core I once saw in China. I grew up under Mao's regime, and we had the Communist dominated education — nationalized testing, nationalized curriculum, and the nationalized indoctrination. So, I grew up in their system. I come to this country for freedom, and I cannot believe this is happening all over again in this country. I don't know what happened to the America — a shining city on a hill for freedom — what's going on in this country?

So, I wanted to let you know to say that when you say, 'Oh, we want our kids to be high scoring on the tests like Chinese kids, they will be global ready, they will be career ready, but I'm telling you, Chinese children are not trained to be independent thinkers. They are trained to be task machines, they are trained to be massive skill workers for corporations, and they have no idea what happened in Tiananmen Square 1989 when Communist government ordered soldiers to shoot its own thousand students. Is this what we want in America?

I understand testing is necessary to improve education, but it's not the way we have now — top down federal government hold the stick, international corporations hold money — okay, we have both carrots and stick to offer to our students. Parents, we're out of carrots. We're supposed to have control of our kids' education, and we have trust our teachers and students and parents to work together — individual rights, individual liberty — that's what I come to this country for.

I don't know if you board members voted for Common Core, to adopt the standards; did you know what's going to happen later? Do you know what's going to be in the U.S. AP History test? American exceptionalism, gone. America's liberty and values of Founding Fathers are gone. Capitalism is gone; only mentioned three times. Is this what we want our kids to be, a task machine — workers, cheap workers — for corporations? No. America is great. Don't compare yourself to China. That's why lots of Chinese, desperate trying to come here to be free, and they all tell you, 'Do not go after Chinese Communist education.' Their system produced great test-takers, great machine workers, but not individuals with critical thinking mind, with interventional skills. They do not challenge their parents, they are brainwashed. I was brainwashed so bad, it took me 10 years in this country to get out of it. So please, look at again Common Core and help us any way you can get out of it.

Listen to what this parent is saying. Common Core is doing the thinking for our kids. It's dumbing them down. They cannot reason anything in their minds. They just acknowledge and agree with what that teacher says.

And what about the teachers? How are they dealing with Common Core?

Stacie Starr, a national award-winning teacher in Ohio, made the painful decision to resign because of Common Core. At a public education forum in her county she said:

When I think about education today, it's very upsetting. We're becoming presenters of materials and not teachers. They've taken away all of our creativity within the classroom between us, as educators, and the students. It's interesting when you ask students to think for themselves; they're so used to material just given to them, given to them, given to them. And you ask them a question to express themselves; they look at you in a robotic look. They cannot think for themselves, and it is really sad.... What I got into education for was to change lives. I wanted to make a difference. I have been able to do that and I cannot do that in the setting in which it is being done right now. I am actually going to resign from teaching after this

year because of what education has become ... We are los-
ing kids ... we're not preparing them for the real world.
Just because they can pass an assessment does not mean
that they are going to be successful in life.

Ms. Starr is not alone. There are many others choosing
to end their teaching careers early because of extra Common
Core duties that eat into a school day — duties that, for some
teachers, include data collection.

SCHOOL DATA SYSTEMS

In a 2009 speech, former U.S. Secretary of Education Arne
Duncan made this statement about student data:

"Hopefully someday we can track children from preschool
to high school and from high school to college and college to
career.... We want to see more states build comprehensive
systems that track students from pre-K through college and
then link school data to workforce data. We want to know
whether Johnny participated in an early learning program and
then completed college on time and whether those things had
any bearing on his earnings as an adult."

According to Jane Robbins, schools that agreed to Common Core (to receive Race To The Top money) also had to
agree to build identical school data systems — identical so
that data could be easily shared — to federal specifications.
Although it has not yet happened, the National Education
Data model would pull data such as disciplinary history, religious affiliation, family income range, and medical history.

Parents who think charter, private, or home schools are the answer should also be aware that Common Core is touching these options as well. Since the primary architect of Common Core, David Coleman, is now the president and CEO of the College Board, the Scholastic Aptitude Test, or SAT, is being revised to align to Common Core. So, students outside of the public school system will have a difficult time passing the SAT without knowing Common Core teaching methods, and acceptance into college is largely based on SAT scores.

What we've entered into is a global school.

YOU ALREADY HAVE COMMUNISM

Progressives such as Barack Obama and Hillary Clinton who are pushing this movement are not looking out for your child because your child is being brainwashed in the public school system to be a compliant, non-thinking citizen. Is that not the fruit of communism?

Remember the sobering words of Nikita Khrushchev: "You Americans are so gullible. No, you won't accept communism outright, but we'll keep feeding you small doses of socialism until you finally wake up and find you already have communism. We won't even have to fight you; we'll so weaken your economy until you'll fall like an overripe fruit into our hands."

Grassroots America has got to stand up and say, "We are not going to accept this. We are not going to have our kids placed under this Common Core agenda." And it is an agenda

— it's a global agenda for our schools, and it's a global agenda for the church.

COMMON CORE FOR THE CHURCH?

The same changes to standards in our public schools — replacing classic literature with government texts; replacing passionate teachers called to educate with "technicians" who distribute information; and replacing true knowledge with test scores — the same things are happening in the church today.

Think about what I am saying. Countless churches have traded the King James Bible for watered down rewrites like *The Message*. Pastors, who are called of God, have switched their message from the Word of God to embrace false doctrines, such as the Purpose-Driven Life and Word of Faith to increase the size and so-called success of their congregations.

This ilk that is in the body of Christ today — this is the Common Core of the church world and it is producing fake Christianity.

And just as students under Common Core will not be properly equipped to face the world, neither will Christians who fail to discern the true gospel of the Lord Jesus Christ and the moving and operation of the Holy Spirit.

Do we have enough Christians left in the world who love the Lord enough to stand up and fight against what's happening in our churches and in our schools?

I pray that we do.

AND SARAH SAW

CHAPTER 9

VAIN IMAGINATIONS

CHAPTER NINE

VAIN IMAGINATIONS

THIS KNOW ALSO, THAT in the last days perilous times shall come. For men shall be lovers of their own selves, covetous, boasters, proud, blasphemers, disobedient to parents, unthankful, unholy, without natural affection, trucebreakers, false accusers, incontinent, fierce, despisers of those that are good, traitors, heady, high-minded, lovers of pleasures more than lovers of God; having a form of godliness, but denying the power thereof: from such turn away (II Tim. 3:1-5).

Two days before the U.S. Supreme Court legalized same-sex marriage in all 50 states, President Obama made this statement in the East Room of the White House at a reception honoring Lesbian, Gay, Bisexual, and Transgender (LGBT) Pride Month:

"In just the past year, America has come far in its acceptance of transgender Americans. And we've got brave folks coming out at the highest levels of business and government, and in sports and in Hollywood. We're seeing television shows portray transgender characters and families. And the power of example is slowly but surely changing people's hearts."

Sadly, the president is right. Acceptance of the transgender lifestyle — and the LGBT agenda — is accelerating in America.

POWER OF EXAMPLE

Transgenders (people who live out a gender identity different from the one they were born with) are quickly growing in number and acceptance as they take their places in the newly defined "civil rights" movement in America, emboldened by that power of example the president mentioned.

More than half of the nation applauded Bruce Jenner's public admission as a transgender — a lifelong transformation, he said, from a male U.S. Olympic champion to the physical appearance of a woman. His decision to share this experience on prime time television was hailed in the media as courageous and heroic.

According to Nielsen ratings, nearly 17 million viewers tuned in to watch Jenner's exclusive interview with Diane Sawyer on ABC's 20/20.

"I would say I have always been confused by my gender identity since I was this big," Jenner said, lowering his hand a few feet from the floor.

Then he gave Sawyer the same explanation that he gave to his own children regarding the struggle with his gender:

"God's looking down, making little Bruce, okay? He's looking down and He says, 'Okay, what are we gonna do with this one? Make him a smart kid, very determined,' and He gave me all of these wonderful qualities. And then at the end, when He's just finishing, He goes, 'Wait a second, we gotta give him something; everybody has stuff in their life they have to deal with, you know? What are we gonna give him?' And God looks down and chuckles a little bit and goes, 'Hey, let's give him the soul of a female, and let's see how he deals with that.'"

Jenner's perception of Almighty God is sad and sarcastic, but, more importantly, it is untrue. God is not confused or spiteful, and neither does He put wrong souls into wrong bodies.

The Bible says, *"God created man in His own image, in the image of God created He him; male and female created He them"* (Gen. 1:27).

Still, Jenner's celebrity status empowered countless others in the transgender community to step out and use the media to tell the positive sides of their stories.

One of the most shocking stories I found in different news sources was about a 7-year-old child who was born a boy, but has been living as a transgender girl since the age of 4. Think of that. The following is an excerpt from this story told in this child's own words on a YouTube video:

When I was born, doctors said I was a boy, but I knew in my heart I was a girl. So I may have some boy body parts, but that's not wrong; that is okay. When I was in preschool, I could play dress-up and I loved it because it made me feel really happy because I got to wear girl dresses so I could just be happy. Sometimes I play like I'm an animal or a ninja or a princess, but that doesn't mean my mom and dad should treat me like it; like it's just make believe. Even though I was a girl, I was afraid to tell my mom and dad because I thought they would not love me anymore and they would throw me out and stop giving me any food or anything. Finally, I had to tell my mom and dad I was a girl because it was just really frustrating that I could not hold it in, and it was so hard to not be who I really was and have them treating me like a boy when I really was a girl. My mom and dad brought me to doctors and the doctor said it would be all okay as long as they let me be a girl. When I started to dress like a girl in preschool, my friends were cool with it, but their parents weren't, and they thought it was contagious like 'transgender pox' or something. I decided to quit preschool because it was better to be myself and lose all my friends than keep pretending. I got to pick new clothes and grow my hair long and my new friends know me as the girl I am in my heart and brain. I did trampoline, gymnastics, dance, 4-H, tae kwon do, Girl Scouts, and more. I'm just a normal girl and I got to dye my hair — three times.

There's still some people that don't understand and are scared because I'm a little bit different, but we want to *fix that*! Some people say that I don't get to go in the right bathroom or go to the right restaurants, but who cares about my body parts? I don't ask what's in *your* underwear! Being transgender is a hard thing, but you can be who you want to be. I'm proud of who I am because I'm transgender and I am a girl. I'm just a normal girl — your average everyday normal transgender girl.

The words of this confused child — and his determination to "fix" the attitudes of those who don't understand his decision to live as a girl — show just how deeply the sin of transgenderism is rooted in this country, ensnaring even our youngest generation.

Yet however positive the confessions of those who defend this gender confusion may be, their stories are in direct conflict with the Word of God.

In Romans 1:21 we read: *"Because that, when they knew God, they glorified him not as God, neither were thankful; but became vain in their imaginations, and their foolish heart was darkened."*

A DIFFERENT STORY

So from a 7-year-old's point of view, living as a transgender may seem elementary, harmless, and easily solved — at that age — by hair dye and girl clothes. But national statistics on transgender life tell a different story.

A national survey of more than 6,000 transgenders from all 50 states revealed these facts:

- Seventy percent of transgenders misuse drugs and alcohol to cope with mistreatment.
- Transgenders are twice as likely to be unemployed.
- Transgenders are twice as likely to be homeless.

- Transgenders live in extreme poverty and are more likely to have incomes under $10,000.
- Forty-one percent of transgenders reported attempting suicide.

Author and public speaker Walt Heyer confirmed these statistics as a recent guest of mine on *Frances & Friends*. Walt spent a good part of his life struggling as a transgender before he came to know Jesus Christ as his personal Lord and Saviour.

On the program, Walt relayed how, as a very small boy, his grandmother would secretly dress him in girl's clothing. For agreeing to wear girl clothes, his grandmother rewarded him with affection and praise. After more than two years of his grandmother cross-dressing him, Walt began to enjoy it and didn't want to lose the love and adoration he received from his grandmother while pretending to be a girl.

But the long-term actions of his grandmother, followed by negative reactions from his family once the secret got out, threw Walt into a tailspin of gender identity issues that lasted for years to come. He continued to cross-dress in secret and "feed this desire that Grandma started."

Walt went on to marry and have two children, but continued to struggle with his sexual identity and with alcohol abuse. In his late 30s, he found a doctor who specialized in gender issues and diagnosed Walt with gender dysphoria. The doctor recommended ongoing hormone therapy and gender reassignment surgery. That same doctor told Walt, "All the stress and confusion will go away. You'll finally be happy in your own skin and you'll be who you really are."

This proved to be a lie.

When Walt did have gender reassignment surgery, he experienced temporary euphoria and relief. But within seven years of his operation, Walt regretted his decision and began to seek ways to change back to his original gender.

"You really don't change," Walt said. "They leave you with a mutilated body. You never became a female. You acted out as though you were when you really weren't. So the change back isn't as dramatic as people think. I'd been living a false gender role like anyone who changes gender."

During his journey back to his original gender, Walt discovered a church that received him in love and a pastor who told him, "My job is to love you. It's God's job to change you."

Praise the Lord, He is able! The Bible says, *"Therefore if any man be in Christ, he is a new creature: old things are passed away; behold, all things are become new"* (II Cor. 5:17).

After a personal encounter with the Lord Jesus Christ, Walt said the Lord redeemed and restored him. Today, he celebrates a stable marriage, has a great relationship with his children, and heads a ministry helping others who struggle with gender identity issues.

SENT TO HEAL THE BROKENHEARTED

There are lot of hurting people out there and I thank God that Walt Heyer shared his story with our SBN viewers and again here for our readers to let people know that there is forgiveness and that you can make the Lord Jesus Christ your personal Saviour and heaven your home. Precious Jesus.

During that show with Walt, I liked what one of our associate pastors, Dave Smith, said about God being the healer of broken hearts. He said, "Whether our hearts are broken because of sins we've committed or because of sins others have committed against us; God is the healer of broken hearts."

We see the Lord Jesus confirming this Himself in the fourth chapter of Luke:

"The Spirit of the Lord is upon Me, because He hath anointed Me to preach the gospel to the poor; He hath sent Me to heal the brokenhearted, to preach deliverance to the captives, and recovering of sight to the blind, to set at liberty them that are bruised, to preach the acceptable year of the Lord" (Lk. 4:18-19).

Brother Smith went on to say that the whole idea of identity comes from God. He said, "There is an answer in Jesus Christ and we can become who He created us to be."

Consider these verses from Psalm 139: *"For You created my inmost being; You knit me together in my mother's womb. I praise You because I am fearfully and wonderfully made; Your works are wonderful, I know that full well."*

Last year, Walt posted a video on YouTube where he said this:

"What I am really troubled by is the universities now are teaching the LGBT multiple gender thing — that gender is fluid. You know, the LGBT is not going to redeem your life; Jesus Christ will. He can redeem yours if you struggle with gender identity issues just like He did mine, and you need to know that."

UNLESS AMERICA REPENTS

I would like to close this article with a message for the church and for this country. It's a few paragraphs taken from a book, *Rape of a Nation*, which my husband wrote in the mid-1980s but is even more relevant today. In fact, we will be re-releasing this book shortly. My husband writes:

> Satan has always endeavored to take God's most cherished creation, mankind, and pervert him to nothing more than the soulless condition of the animal kingdom.
>
> Because of their great wickedness, God destroyed Sodom and Gomorrah. If necessary, He will destroy our nation if men refuse to repent and turn from their wicked ways. But, in a greater sense, Sodom and Gomorrah were destroyed because of the shortfall in the number of righteous people. If there had been just 10 righteous people, God would have spared these cities.
>
> We, the people of God, can't ignore the cascade of filth being poured out upon us from the pit of hell. Sexual immorality, pornography, sexual abuse of children, and homosexuality all reflect the depths of depravity to which America has sunk.
>
> Alexis de Tocqueville's famous words ring with profound truth: 'America is great because she is good. If America

ceases to be good, America will cease to be great.'

America is being weighed in the balance and found wanting. The sexual revolution drains its poisonous consequences across the land like a pustulant sore. Unless America repents, the fate of Sodom and Gomorrah will surely overtake *us*.

In the book of Malachi, the Lord says that if we will return to Him, He will return to us. Let this promise be our prayer for the United States of America.

AND SARAH SAW

LET NO MAN PUT ASUNDER

LET NO MAN PUT ASUNDER

AND HE ANSWERED AND said unto them, Have ye not read, that he which made them at the beginning made them male and female, and said, For this cause shall a man leave father and mother, and shall cleave to his wife: and they twain shall be one flesh? Wherefore they are no more twain, but one flesh. What therefore God hath joined together, let not man put asunder (Mat. 19:4-6).

On June 26, 2015, the U.S. Supreme Court ruled in *Obergefell v. Hodges*, declaring that state-level bans on same-sex marriage are unconstitutional. Moments after the decision was announced, President Obama made a personal cell phone call to the lead plaintiff in the case, Jim Obergefell.

After offering his congratulations and praising Obergefell's leadership, the president told him:

Not only have you been a great example for people, but you're also going to bring about lasting change in this country. It's pretty rare when that happens, so I couldn't be prouder of you and your husband, and God bless you.

Ladies and gentlemen, God is not going to bless any part of this court's decision because it was made in complete and utter disobedience to the Word of God.

NOT A CIVIL RIGHTS STRUGGLE

In a message preached over the Fourth of July weekend at Family Worship Center, Donnie did an excellent job of dealing with this subject of same-sex marriage.

He said, "It's not a civil rights struggle. It is a moral problem. It's not political. It's not constitutional. It is a *moral* problem that defines who we are as a nation and how far we have sunk as a people."

We don't believe that it's right for the U.S. Supreme Court or anybody else to try and redefine marriage as something other than what God says it is. In the book of Genesis, we see that marriage is the first institution that God ever created:

'And the LORD God caused a deep sleep to fall upon Adam, and he slept (records the first anesthesia): *and He took one of his ribs* (the word rib here actually means 'side'), *and closed up the flesh instead thereof* (the woman is not merely of a rib, but actually of one side of man);

And the rib (side), *which the LORD God had taken from man, made He a woman* (the Hebrew says, 'built He a woman'; Horton says, 'When God created the man, the word form was used, which is the same word used of a potter forming a clay jar; but the word build here seems to mean God paid even more attention to the creation of the woman'), *and brought her unto the man* (presents a formal presentation, with God, in essence, performing the first wedding; thus He instituted the bonds of the marriage covenant, which is actually called the covenant of God [Prov. 2:17], indicating that God is the Author of this sacred institution; this is the marriage model and was instituted by God; any other model, such as homosexual marriages, so-called, can be constituted as none other than an abomination in the eyes of God [Rom. 1:24-28])' (Gen. 2:21-22, The Expositor's Study Bible).

MAIN SOURCE OF SUPPORT

This is what the Word of God says, but it's not what people want to believe, especially America's young people. Just weeks before the Supreme Court ruled on same-sex marriage, we sent a TV crew from SonLife Broadcasting Network to the streets of Baton Rouge to ask random people for their definition of marriage.

Nearly all of the people we interviewed — middle-aged and up — said that they believed marriage was between a man and a woman, but take a look at the responses we received from the younger set, roughly 25 years old and younger:

Q: How do you define marriage?

A: I think marriage is love between two people, and it doesn't matter what two people it is.

A: I'm open-minded. I have a lot of gay friends, and I've never seen anything wrong with it. Traditionally, I guess it's the union of a man and a woman but to me, I think it's just the union of two people that love each other.

A: Our generation is known for doing things completely different and I think [traditional marriage] is out of date;
[same-sex marriage] is a new thing that's happening, and we
should all accept it and not judge.

A: Anybody who wants to have same-sex marriage or
anything, I feel like that's your choice, and I don't think anyone should judge somebody for that. I think whatever you
feel like you want to do, you should do.

The responses of these young people are not surprising.
In June 2015, a Pew Research Center's report pointed to
youth as a major source of support for same-sex marriage.

The report states:

"A key component of the shifting attitudes on this issue
is the strong support for gay rights among younger Americans. Younger generations have long been more accepting
of homosexuality and of same-sex marriage than older generations, and as millennials (who are currently ages 18-34)
have entered adulthood, those views have influenced overall
public opinion."

CHANGE OF HEART

At 31 years old, Heather Barwick qualifies as a millen-
nial and, as the daughter of lesbian parents, she grew up as an
advocate and supporter of gay marriage. But somewhere into
her 20s, she said she could no longer be a supporter because
"of the nature of the same-sex relationship itself."

Barwick, now a wife and mother of four, is a children's

rights activist. In March 2015, she wrote an open letter entitled, "Dear Gay Community: Your Kids Are Hurting," to
explain her change of heart. Barwick wrote:

> It's only with some time and distance from my childhood
> that I'm able to reflect on my experiences and recognize
> the long-term consequences that same-sex parenting had
> on me.... And it's only now, as I watch my children loving
> and being loved by their father each day, that I can see the
> beauty and wisdom in traditional marriage and parent-
> ing. Same-sex marriage and parenting withholds either a
> mother or father from a child while telling him or her that
> it doesn't matter. That it's all the same. But it's not. A lot
> of us, a lot of your kids, are hurting. My father's absence
> created a huge hole in me, and I ached every day for a dad.
> I loved my mom's partner, but another mom could never
> have replaced the father I lost.

For other children of same-sex couples, the damage is
even greater.

Before the Supreme Court's ruling, B. N. Klein was one
of four adult children of gay parents who testified against
same-sex marriage at the 5th Circuit Court of Appeals and
reportedly argued that "government-sanctioned homosexual
unions could lead to disaster for thousands of kids."

In her brief to the court Klein wrote:

"While I do not believe all gays would be de facto bad
parents, I know that the gay community has never in my
lifetime put children first as anything other than a piece of

property, a past mistake, or a political tool to be dressed up and taken out as part of a dog-and-pony show to impress the well-meaning."

Klein's brief also stated that as a child of a lesbian mother, she was pressured to pay "constant homage and attention" to her mother's gay identity, taught that "some Jews and most Christians are stupid and hate gays and are violent," and told that homosexuals were "much more creative and artistic because they are not repressed and are naturally more *feeling*."

Katy Faust was another one of these four adult children who testified saying:

"The label of bigot or hater has become very powerful and effective tools to silence those of us who choose not to endorse the marriage platform of many gay lobbyists. For much of my adult life, I was content to keep my opinions on the subject of marriage to myself. I was (and still am) sickened by the accusation that I was bigoted and anti-gay for my belief in natural marriage."

Faust said she was speaking out now because she believes that a child has the right to a mother and a father:

> When we institutionalize same-sex marriage...we move from permitting citizens the freedom to live as they choose, to promoting same-sex headed households.... Now we are normalizing a family structure where a child will always be deprived daily of one gender influence and the relationship with at least one natural parent. Our cultural narrative becomes one that, in essence, tells children that they have no right

to the natural family structure or their biological parents, but that children simply exist for the satisfaction of adult desires.

Dawn Stefanowicz, who was raised by a homosexual father who later died of AIDS, testified against same-sex marriage in her native Canada, which legalized gay marriage in July 2005.

According to Stefanowicz, Canada has changed a lot in those 10 years. She said that as soon as same-sex marriage passed in her country, parenting was immediately redefined.

Stefanowicz wrote: "Necessary parental rights to teach children your beliefs, express your opinions, and practice your personal faith are infringed upon by the state when your beliefs, opinions, and or faith practices are in opposition to what is taught and promoted at school. In fact, in Ontario, Canada, the Human Rights Commission regulations permeate and surround all public education."

Think of that.

I thank the Lord that these people were brave enough to come forward and speak out on this issue. Their testimonies illustrate the impact that same-sex marriage is having on our children, schools, and our nation.

REPETITION REDUCES RESISTANCE

Still, the Lesbian, Gay, Bisexual, and Transgender (LGBT) community remains unsatisfied and continues their fight for what they call "civil rights."

We see their agenda unfolding every day in the news: the Boy Scouts welcoming openly gay men and boys; Baylor University–a prominent Christian college in this country — dropping the phrase "homosexual acts" from its sexual misconduct policy; an Oregon labor commissioner ordering Christian bakers to pay $135,000 for refusing to bake a cake for a same-sex wedding.

On *Frances & Friends*, Mike Muzzerall commented on this type of progression.

"What happens is, if we're in a situation where we're tolerant — we're not abusive toward the person, but we don't acknowledge it — that's no longer good enough," he said. "Now they want us to accept. Repetition reduces resistance. We're seeing it everywhere, and it's wearing us down as a church, and we need to stand on what the Word of God says."

Pastor Mike is absolutely right.

The Bible says, *"What therefore God hath joined together, let not man put asunder."*

What authority does the U.S. Supreme Court have to change the definition of marriage?

They don't.

Four of the justices disagreed with the majority on that historic ruling, including Associate Justice Samuel Alito, who offered America a warning.

In his dissent Alito wrote:

> Today's decision usurps the constitutional right of the people to decide whether to keep or alter the traditional understanding of marriage. The decision

will also have other important consequences. It will be used to vilify Americans who are unwilling to assent to the new orthodoxy. In the course of its opinion, the majority compares traditional marriage laws to laws that denied equal treatment for African-Americans and women. The implications of this analogy will be exploited by those who are determined to stamp out every vestige of dissent.

JUDGMENT AND THE CROSS

On the same night of this ruling, President Obama decided to illuminate the White House in rainbow colors, symbolizing gay pride. Outraged by this demonstration, Rev. Franklin Graham posted, "God is the one who gave the rainbow, and it was associated with His judgment. God sent a flood to wipe out the entire world because mankind had become so wicked and violent."

Ladies and gentlemen, as my husband has said so many times, "The only thing holding back that judgment and wrath of Almighty God is the Cross of Christ."

If the church is not preaching the Cross, then judgment comes.

AND
SARAH
SAW

THE BIBLICAL VIEW
OF HOMOSEXUALITY

THE BIBLICAL VIEW
OF HOMOSEXUALITY

FOR THIS CAUSE GOD gave them up unto vile affections: for even their women did change the natural use into that which is against nature: And likewise also the men, leaving the natural use of the woman, burned in their lust one toward another; men with men working that which is unseemly, and receiving in themselves that recompence of their error which was meet (Rom. 1:26-27).

After reading a vast variety of emails, articles, news clips, etc., I feel strongly impressed by the Holy Spirit to address the very delicate and controversial issue of homosexuality. And not only homosexuality as society knows it to be, but also God's biblical standard concerning it.

I do not wish to speak from standards of my own making here or the ethical standards of our modern culture, but from the standards of a Holy God who has asked me to reach out to all who will hear Him concerning this very critical issue of our time. I hope to make it clear to you how the Lord feels about homosexuality and, as well, His solution for this terrible sin.

I once heard a wise man say that while God is the greatest embodiment of love that has ever existed or will ever exist, it is not love that makes Him God. God is God because of His power. He is God because of His authority. He is all-powerful, all-mighty, and all-knowing. Yes, God is love, but love is not God. The love of God is holy. This presents a problem for a fallen, sinful creation.

Mankind cannot receive the love of God without willingly submitting to His order and authority by the way of the Cross. The sacrifice of His Son, Jesus, for the redemption of our sins was God's way of showing us that within His great power was also great love. But, the conditions inherent in this way of the Cross must be met for a man to receive the love of God on a personal basis — to receive salvation. We must make Jesus both our Saviour and our Lord.

Therefore, the way of the Cross requires a man to surrender lordship of his own life to God, and he must also agree with God that it is His standards alone that constitute holiness. Therefore, if God deems anything to be sin, man must agree. It is not man's right to make the distinction between right and wrong; that is His right as Lord.

His Spirit is, in fact, speaking continually to the hearts of men: *"I am the Lord."*

We are without excuse.

"And God said unto Moses, I AM THAT I AM: and He said, Thus shall you say unto the children of Israel, I AM has sent me unto you" (Ex. 3:14).

THE WORD *HOMOSEXUALITY*

Many today would try to argue that we can't be sure how the Lord views homosexuality because the specific word *homosexuality* is not found in Scripture.

However, this argument is completely foolish because the Bible does use plenty of other words and phrases that mean precisely the same thing. Besides, the word *homosexuality* did not even enter the English vocabulary until the early 20th century.

It is, in fact, for this peculiar sin that God destroyed Sodom and Gomorrah, giving the word *sodomy* its biblical origin. In ecclesiastical Latin, *sodomy* is translated "peccatum Sodomiticum," or the "sin of Sodom."

"But the men of Sodom were wicked and sinners before the Lord *exceedingly"* (Gen. 13:13).

"Then the Lord *rained upon Sodom and upon Gomorrah brimstone and fire from the* Lord *out of heaven; And He overthrew those cities, and all the plain, and all the inhabitants of the cities, and that which grew upon the ground"* (Gen. 19:24-25).

"There shall be no whore of the daughters of Israel, nor a sodomite of the sons of Israel" (Deut. 23:17).

"And there were also sodomites in the land: and they did according to all the abominations of the nations which the Lord *cast out before the children of Israel"* (I Ki. 14:24).

"And he broke down the houses of the sodomites, who were by the house of the Lord*"* (II Ki. 23:7).

THE MEANING OF HOMOSEXUALITY

Also, referring specifically to homosexual acts, Leviticus 18:22 says: *"You shall not lie with mankind, as with womankind: it is abomination."* Leviticus 20:13 says: *"If a man also lie with mankind, as he lies with a woman, both of them have committed an abomination: they shall surely be put to death; their blood shall be upon them."*

And perhaps the most obvious evidence that the Lord opposes homosexuality is that it is simply unnatural. It clearly goes against His intention as Creator because it goes against the natural sexual expression of human beings.

It also tears down the spiritual type the Lord intended for marriage to display. God created marriage as a covenant relationship between a man and woman as a picture of the covenant relationship a believer enters into with the Lord when he is born again.

A Christian becomes one with Christ as a husband and wife become one. The family unit then becomes a means of protection, security, and love, which demonstrates the very provision the Lord provides for His children.

"And the rib, which the LORD God had taken from man, made He a woman, and brought her unto the man. And Adam said, This is now bone of my bones, and flesh of my flesh: she shall be called woman, because she was taken out of man. Therefore shall a man leave his father and his mother, and shall cleave unto his wife: and they shall be one flesh" (Gen. 2:22-24).

I Corinthians 6:9 uses the word *effeminate,* which is a Greek word specifically meaning "sodomite" or "male homosexual prostitute." It does not merely refer to a man with feminine qualities like we use it today.

I Timothy 1:10 uses the phrase, *"Them that defile themselves with mankind."*

The Greek word used in this verse is *arsenokoitais* and means "male homosexuals."

Referring back to I Corinthians 6:9, this same Greek word was also originally used in place of the phrase *"abusers of themselves with mankind."*

Therefore, *arsenokoites* more specifically refers to "abusers" or "to be guilty of unnatural offenses; a sodomite; a homosexual; a sex pervert." The Holy Spirit here likens homosexuality to predatorial abuse, even the abuse of oneself.

THE GREATEST SIN?

Yet today in city after city there are entire areas given over to the homosexual lifestyle. The acceptance of this practice in modern society has been gradually building for sometime now, but in the last several years, we have seen an explosion in its growth as the minds of reprobate men fail to understand its far-reaching consequences.

With this delusion has also come the demand for the approval, inclusion, and support of homosexual rights. The demand is harsh and determined, and it is not only coming from homosexuals, but from our very own government.

They press on, despite the fact that, historically-speaking, every time a city was inflicted with this vice and left to run its natural course, the city became so shaken that it crumbled and fell. Homosexual practice is, in fact, widely recognized as one of the causes for the downfall of the Roman Empire.

They destroyed themselves by their own perversion, similar to ancient civilizations that literally sacrificed themselves out of existence. This is exactly what we are facing today in the United States. From this point on, every decision we make concerning the issue of homosexuality will have lasting effects on our survival, not only as a nation, but as a human race.

In times past, it was only particular segments of the world that were permeated with this vile sin and destroyed. Today, because it is embraced worldwide, the entire global community stands to be judged. This is absolutely one of the greatest signs of the times before us. Get ready, saints, for our *"redemption draweth nigh."*

THE TRUTH

It is evident that intolerance and outrage are already coming from both sides of the fence in America. The battle cry has been sounded, the fight has been started, and the stones have been thrown.

Indeed, the nation is once again divided, and the war for the soul of America has begun! So, how should a Christian fight? We certainly do not fight with hate because it is not the sinner whom God hates; rather, it is his sin. It is homosexuality that we are against, not the homosexual. A true Christian will do everything possible to show a homosexual the love of God and the way of the Cross, for he realizes that he was also once lost in his sin.

We also welcome any homosexual to come to Family Worship Center as long as he conducts himself properly and does not disrupt the service in any way (which are the same requirements we have for everyone who attends our services).

We look at our church as a hospital; it is there so the sick may receive healing. Just understand, though, that we will preach the truth regarding sin. A true Christian can never fail to tell the homosexual the truth about his sin, no matter how much others may misinterpret the attitude of his heart. Love does not lie.

The apostle Paul once asked, *"Am I therefore become your enemy, because I tell you the truth?"* (Gal. 4:16).

SEXUAL PREFERENCE

Under a distorted version of what some homosexual activists are calling freedom, there is a movement taking place today that is designed to convince the American people that homosexuality is normal and that the homosexual's perverse practices are only a matter of sexual preference — something to be seen as perfectly natural and non-threatening.

But, if everyone practiced this lifestyle, we would quickly see the extinction of the human race. How can we simply call normal or natural any so-called preference that puts man on the endangered species list?

It doesn't even adhere to America's Declaration of Independence, which was written to guarantee us "life, liberty, and the pursuit of happiness."

How can we have life without procreation?

On a spiritual level, the reality is that Satan despises the fact that man has been favored by God. The Devil's wish is to destroy His highest creation.

Homosexuality is the Devil's most conscientious effort to eliminate the human race. It not only stops procreation, but it destroys the family unit.

Already, more than one spouse has been abandoned due to unnatural lust, and more than one marriage was forsaken before it ever took place at all. Homosexuality is, thereby, demonic in nature as unclean spirits aid Satan's goal to *"steal, kill, and destroy"* (Jn. 10:10).

THE LAW

Of course, laws cannot put a person in right standing with God because the problem is more than ethical, it is spiritual, but laws help guide society as a whole. This is why it is important for Christians to vote in the right laws for our country and speak out as much as possible.

However, this is also why homosexual advocates are pressuring the Christian community, as well as the heterosexual community in general, to cater to the homosexual agenda in every way possible.

In the meantime, our minds are being desensitized by the media. Every time we turn around, we find that a homosexual character in a story is also the hero of the story, or another one of our favorite celebrities unashamedly announces his homosexuality. We laugh at their jokes and admire their talents, but what we forget is that the homosexual community will not stop until it becomes a crime in America for anyone to call a homosexual act a sin.

In fact, we just recently saw another major step in this direction. Bill HR 2015 (a.k.a. the Employment Non-Discrimination Act), which prevents employers from refusing to hire someone based on actual or perceived sexual orientation, just passed the House.

Most of the time America's citizens are denied the chance to speak out against the homosexual agenda, and those who try are quickly labeled as homophobic, narrow-minded, and ignorant.

But, may we not force our moral and spiritual conscience to take a backseat because we fear our peers and the labels they may give us. If homosexuals can "come out of the closet," so must we. Christians claim to be people of faith, but remember that James said it well, *"Faith without works is dead"* (James 2:26).

THE RIGHT SPIRIT

Also, contrary to popular opinion, it is possible for a person to speak out against homosexuality and vote against homosexual agendas without hating the homosexual or treating him harshly in any way. Anyone who does such is not dealing with the issue with a correct spirit or attitude.

And, so-called Christians who do such are actually hurting the cause of Christ.

Yet organizations are being formed today that wish to label anyone who will clearly speak the truth according to the Bible, as a "religious bigot." For example, one organization called Faith In America is actively holding educational campaigns across America. They state on their website, "The fundamental mission of Faith In America is to end bigotry disguised as religious truth and in doing so, ensure full and equal civil rights for the lesbian, gay, bisexual and transgender community in America."

These organizations try to put homosexuality in the same category as race or gender. But the two are not comparable because the Bible does not label race or gender as sin like it does homosexuality.

Actually, Christians cannot accurately be called bigots because the definition of a bigot includes prejudice. Prejudice cannot exist in the proper understanding that the ground is level at the foot of the Cross.

The only thing the true Christian is against is sin.

AND SARAH SAW

CHAPTER 12

THAT WHICH
IS UNSEEMLY

THAT WHICH IS UNSEEMLY

ONE OF THE STRONGEST agenda items pushed by the homosexual community to the church today is the attempt to "Christianize" homosexuality. This can only pervert God's Word. In fact, the concept of Christianizing anything is really unscriptural.

A truly redeemed person can accurately be called a Christian, but no person, behavior, culture, or institution of this world can be Christianized — conformed into Christlikeness — by man. Ultimately, the effort will fail because it is only the Cross of Christ that negated the effects of the fall.

All of creation was corrupted as a result of Adam's sin, but the Cross was a work done for the souls of men, not for the systems and lifestyles of men. When a man's soul has been cleansed by the blood, he will no longer desire to live according to his fallen nature.

The homosexual, therefore, cannot claim his behavior conforms to Christianity just because the relationship with his partner is monogamous.

In this chapter, we will look at some of the history of

homosexuality so that the reader will be able to quickly see that it is totally incompatible with Christianity. A true Christian does not have the need to Christianize his life.

THE BIBLE DOES NOT AGREE

To begin with, it is actually quite ironic that many homosexuals accuse religious communities of being their greatest enemies because the true origins of homosexuality are very closely tied to religion.

At one time, religion was their greatest friend. The earliest accounts of homosexual behavior are, in fact, found within the confines of the ancient pagan religions. And, if you look closely, you can see that this association has subtly carried on to this very day.

Most modern homosexuals consider themselves to be spiritually gifted in one way or another. Perhaps this is why it angers them so much to discover that the Bible does not agree. It is here that we begin to see that there is a vast difference between Christianity and the other religions of the world.

Pagan religiosity can bend, evolve, and recreate itself to fit any time or place, but Christianity has always had the supernatural strength of the Lord to remain separate, different, and undefiled.

WORSHIP?

Unredeemed humanity began the worship of many gods,

which we call polytheism, very early in human history. The various gods were both male and female, and unlike the one true God of the Bible, these pagan gods acted in much the same way as humans, with perhaps the most obvious being that they had sexual relations with one another and procreated.

Logically, the ancient pagan worshippers also associated these gods with survival needs, such as fertility, agriculture, and war. In the attempt to ensure they would receive these necessary blessings, they tried to venerate the gods by appealing to their nature.

This makes sense; it has been said that imitation is the highest form of flattery. If we want the approval of a particular group, we demonstrate our respect for them by acting the same way they do. We might also imitate them because we desire to have the same power we perceive belongs to them. So, since the ancient groups believed in sexually active gods, they included sexual activity as part of their worship. There is even evidence that the pagan priests themselves (who were often believed to stand in the place of gods on earth) facilitated or participated in the sexual arousal of their worship:

In his article, "Judaism's Sexual Revolution: Why Judaism (and then Christianity) Rejected Homosexuality," Dennis Prager wrote: "Given the sexual activity of the gods, it is not surprising that the religions themselves were replete with all forms of sexual activity. In the Near East, and elsewhere, virgins were deflowered by priests prior to engaging in relations with their husbands, and sacred or ritual prostitution was almost universal."

SYMBOLS OF MALE WORSHIP

Homosexual activity, it appears, came to be viewed as means of obtaining extra fertility. Male gods were considered more productive than female gods because they were the ones with the ability to plant seeds. Therefore, it became very important to invoke the male gods to keep the earth, which was considered female, fertile. Worship practices included allowing men to spill semen on the earth.

In fact, it was this theory among paganism that began tendencies toward male superiority in many religions. Christianity is falsely accused of such. Early pagan temples were designed to serve as male phallic symbols. As early as ancient Babylon, ziggurat towers were used for the worship of the gods. Sadly, we can still find these symbols of male-worship today, such as the obelisk in the Vatican Square at Rome, the Washington Monument, and Cleopatra's Needles, which are a trio of obelisks inscribed with Egyptian hieroglyphics and located in London, Paris, and New York City.

IDOLATRY

The Greeks admired the physical body, especially the male body. The worship of Adonis, who was also the Phoenician deity Tammuz, included homosexual activity.

Supposedly, the perfect dimensions and beauty of his body was an ideal worthy of godhood. Adonis is still referred to in the erotic literature of the homosexual community today.

This Greek worship of body image has carried on even into our modern culture, both among heterosexuals and homosexuals. Clearly, its pagan roots have never produced good fruit. The idolatry of our own beauty has brought us to the point of total corruption. It is amazing how often religious man ultimately worships himself.

"But became vain in their imaginations ... Professing themselves to be wise, they became fools, And changed the glory of the uncorruptible God into an image made like to corruptible man ... And worshipped and served the creature more than the Creator ... For this cause God gave them up unto vile affections: for even their women did change the natural use into that which is against nature" (Rom. 1:21-26).

We must always remember that idolatry is actually committed in the heart; we don't have to literally bow before an image to worship it.

HOMOSEXUAL ACTIVITY

It is interesting that even though homosexual activity was considered a perfectly normal way to appreciate the created human form or engage in erotic pleasures, exclusive homosexuality was not acceptable. A Greek man should have also been attracted to women. In order to meet his obligation to contribute to the continuation of their society, a male would be expected to marry and establish a family by a certain point in his life.

"The education of children, however, was taken care of by the state. This did not include girls because they were really only valued for procreation purposes. The educational system was designed to teach boys how to be men.

And yes, homosexual conduct was part of this education process because it was the primary goal of the teacher to gain the admiration and respect of the student. This way the boy would grow up with a fierce attachment and submission to his leaders.

Likewise, in the Greek military, homosexual activity was encouraged as a sort of male bonding. It was believed that they would fight harder to protect the other men in their unit if it included men with whom they had been intimate.

The only thing the Greek military would not tolerate was a man who was always passive in homosexual activity. He would actually be expelled from service because he had supposedly become polluted — too much like a woman — and could no longer be trusted to protect his brothers.

To make a long story short, the Greeks used perverse sexual abuse to ensure loyalty within their ranks and control the members of their society.

THE IDEA OF CONTROL

Much like the Greeks, the Romans allowed all kinds of sexual practices — both heterosexual and homosexual — for pleasure, just as long as order in the society was maintained.

They would only be criticized for their sexual liaisons if they caused disturbances in the home and, thus, in the society. Fourteen of the first 15 emperors were said to be homosexual.

Actually, most of Roman society was heavily influenced by the Greeks; Roman gods were virtually the same gods as the Greek gods, just with Latin names.

One difference was that the Romans believed it was the father's responsibility to train the children, so at least the sexual abuse was not quite as rampant in the Roman education system. Moral restriction in regard to sexuality occurred based on the idea of control.

Those who allowed themselves to be controlled by their partners, even if it only meant submission to the partners' desires, were considered weak and valueless to society.

Class distinctions often played a role as well. It was considered appropriate for someone of a higher social standing to require sex of a slave or woman, but a free Roman man should not have to submit to another man.

How unlike the God of the Bible this is! The Lord placed sex within the confines of marriage, where a man and wife submit to each other in love. Sexuality was created as an expression of love, not control.

ANDROGYNY

In ancient Egypt, the gods were often depicted as androgynous beings, meaning they were both male and female or that their sexual identity was ambiguous. In practice, they would be considered bisexual.

The Egyptian Pharaoh, Akhenaten, was depicted in artwork as multi-gendered. Supposedly, he only allowed the worship of Alton, who was an androgynous god.

The religious philosophy of alchemy was practiced in ancient Egypt and probably connected with the prominence of such gender-blending. Alchemy's goal is the blending of all elements or parts, including extreme opposites, into a divine "elixir of life" that will bring about a sort of transformation into immortality or godhood. So, androgyny was highly respected, and apparently, it is also celebrated in modern times.

Although it manifests more in regard to gender roles, we love to see the sexes switch traditional activities or boundaries. We applaud working women, stay-at-home dads, and especially transgender fashion trends. Even modern psychology teaches that everyone has a touch of the opposite gender in their unconscious mind, and that tapping into it may bring someone newfound enlightenment upon his view on the world.

JUDAISM

Indeed, from Babylon to Rome, and even to modern secular culture, the pagan gods and goddesses have pursued any and every aspect of sexuality possible. But, this clearly reveals just what an amazing impact the one true God would have on the world. Judaism, and then a thousand years later, Christianity would be a lighthouse of freedom from indescribable amounts of perversity and sin.

In the earlier mentioned article, Dennis Prager addressed this as well.

He writes, "The first thing Judaism did was to desexualize God. 'In the beginning, God created the heavens and the earth' by his will, not through any sexual behavior. This broke with all other religions, and it alone changed human history."

Prager also mentions how Judaism places controls on sexual activity.

"It could no longer dominate religion and social life," he writes. "It was to be sanctified — which in Hebrew means 'separated' — from the world and placed in the home, in the bed of husband and wife. Judaism's restricting of sexual behavior was one of the essential elements that enabled society to progress ... [Producing] the most far-reaching changes in history."

We can clearly see that today in America, some very deliberate attempts to reverse such historical progress are being made. In the book, *The Homosexual Agenda: Exposing the Principal Threat to Religious Freedom Today,* two homosexual activists, Marshall Kirk and Hunter Madsen, laid out a detailed plan using persuasion and marketing techniques:

"We have in mind a strategy as calculated and powerful as that which gays are accused of employing by their enemies. It's time to learn from Madison Avenue to roll out the big guns. Gays must launch a large-scale campaign to reach straights through the mainstream media. We're talking about propaganda."

Their book also made this statement: "The strategy was sixfold: talk about gays and gayness as loudly and often as possible, portray gays as victims instead of aggressive challengers, give homosexual protectors a just cause, make gays look good, make the victimizers look bad, and solicit funds (get corporate America and major foundations to financially support the homosexual cause)."

TAKE A STAND!

The Metropolitan Community Church now has at least 300 churches and affiliated groups in 22 countries around the world. They help to sponsor a large billboard campaign.

Each billboard displays the question, "Would Jesus Discriminate?" in an attempt to justify the homosexual agenda with Scripture. But every Scripture they use has been twisted with an evil lie designed to cause doubt in what the Bible has already proclaimed as sin.

Propaganda campaigns such as this one have actually made quite a bit of progress. Remember, the Employment Non-Discrimination Act (Bill H.R.3685) is making its rounds through Congress, having already passed the House on November 7, 2007.

It provides employment protections similar to those of the Civil Rights Act of 1964, but specifically applies to gay, lesbian, bisexual, and under HR 2015, transgender employees.

Thank the Lord that some congregations are not giving in to the pressure of their peers. They are taking a stand and counting the cost.

Christ Church in Watertown, Connecticut, will separate from the national Episcopal church and go by a new name: New Hope Anglican Church. Rev. Allyn Benedict, among many other rectors, did not approve the naming of an openly gay man, V. Gene Robinson, bishop of New Hampshire.

Benedict and other Christ Church leaders felt that the national church rejected scriptural authority and traditions of the church. *Hartford Courant* staffer Kate Melone wrote, "In cutting affiliation with the national leaders, the congregation has agreed to give up its church buildings and property, estimated to be worth $7 million, and its name, Christ Church Parish."

GUILT

There is one more aspect regarding homosexuality's connection to religion and spirituality that we should seriously consider.

A homosexual may make religion a priority out of a desperate need to alleviate the guilt under which he lives. Anyone living in dire sin will try to ease his conscience by some means, whether he realizes what he is doing or not.

A homosexual's desire to be heavily involved in a church or religious organization may be quite strong because, in all reality, he fears death. He is not really sure he will make it to heaven, and so, if he thinks he has the approval of Christian brethren, he may feel a little bit safer. This is another reason why true Christians must understand the responsibility they have to discern and speak the truth in love.

God help us not to give anyone a false hope.

AND SARAH SAW

CHAPTER 13

ALCOHOL:
THE GREAT DECEIVER

ALCOHOL: THE GREAT DECEIVER

RECENTLY ON *FRANCES & FRIENDS* we discussed a topic that I believe bears repeating — it is the subject of alcohol. I opened our show by reading this email:

> On your program, you got on the subject of alcohol again, and I wonder why this is such a big issue to you. I never drank and I have no desire to, but almost every Christian has an occasional glass of wine.
>
> My husband was told by his doctor to have a glass of wine each night to help his heart. The Bible doesn't discourage drinking in moderation, so why do you keep harping on it? Even the extremely conservative Protestant Reformation churches here call wine, 'a gift from God.'
>
> I don't drink, so I'm not trying to justify it. I just think it's quite legalistic to condemn something that the Bible doesn't condemn. Drunkenness is another matter though entirely.

WHAT IS THE HARM?

While that email went on to address other topics, I want to deal with these comments made about alcohol because they come up again and again from our audience. One point the email addressed concerns Christians and social drinking. Just what is the harm in a Christian drinking one glass of wine on a holiday or special occasion?

I liked how our panelist, Jim Nations, responded to this issue. As one of our associate pastors here at the ministry, Jim does quite a bit of counseling on this topic, and he was quick to mention Proverbs 20:1, quoted here from The Expositor's Study Bible: *"Wine is a mocker, strong drink is raging: and whosoever is deceived thereby is not wise.* (The Holy Spirit here says that 'wine mocks,' and it causes a 'raging' in the hearts and lives of all who imbibe. As well, it is a great 'deceiver.' This means that every believer ought to be a teetotaler.)"

Think about what the Holy Spirit is saying to us in this verse of Scripture. As Christians, we should not be deceived by the mockery of alcohol because its use causes so much hurt and pain to people. As Jim went on to say, "No one starts out as a drunk; they start out with a drink."

ALCOHOL SHATTERS LIVES

That's why we will continue to address the problem of alcohol, even when others perceive our stand against it as judgmental. I think that instead of being judgmental, what we're doing is looking at the facts. It is well known that drunk driving has killed maybe more people than anything else. In 2010, more than 10,000 people died in alcohol-impaired driving crashes, according to the National Highway Traffic Safety Administration. That's one death every 51 minutes.

Just recently, I read stories of two lovely Christian families who had their lives literally shattered because of drunk drivers who either killed or maimed members of their families, affecting these precious people for the rest of their lives.

Tragedies like these started with one drink or one glass of wine. I'm sure it makes little difference to families who have suffered such painful losses to know that the person who killed their loved one was a social drinker or a hard-core drunkard. Too many of us hear these numbers and shrug our shoulders, but we are talking about death — death!

Many of the people who died in alcohol-related car crashes did not know Jesus Christ as their personal Saviour. How can a Christian condone anything that causes souls to be lost to an eternal hell?

According to Scripture, believers have a responsibility. We are not to cause others to stumble. We *are* our brother's keeper. So even if *you* can have one drink and stop, you don't know who will not be able to stop. You don't know who will become the next alcoholic or drunk driver, so your social or moderate drinking is actually quite unloving. According to the Bible, you do not love your brother: *"And whosoever shall offend one of these little ones who believe in Me, it is better for him that a millstone were hanged about his neck, and he were cast into the sea"* (Mk. 9:42).

That email also stated, "The Bible doesn't discourage drinking in moderation," but I beg to differ. The Bible certainly does not encourage moderate drinking! In fact, there are many warnings in Scripture regarding alcohol.

HIS COLOUR IN THE CUP

One verse says not to even look at wine. In other words, don't even consider it: *"Who has woe? who has sorrow? who has contentions? who has babbling? who has wounds without cause? who has redness of eyes? They that tarry long at the wine; they who go to seek mixed wine. Look not you upon the wine when it is red, when it gives his colour in the cup, when it moves itself aright. At the last it bites like a serpent, and stings like an adder. Your eyes shall behold strange women, and your heart shall utter perverse things"* (Prov. 23:29-33).

Alcohol is like any other sin — it gets a hold on you. First, you take one drink; then, two makes you feel better, and then three makes you feel even more carefree. Before you know it, you're keeping a bottle hidden in your work desk, at home, or purchasing it on airplanes when you fly. Once addicted to alcohol, you find ways to get it.

Alcohol is a serious, serious problem and addiction. We have people out there who are struggling within an inch of taking their own lives because of this sin that so many others are trying to justify.

The seriousness of alcohol use becomes very clear when you get an email from a self-described alcoholic ready to take his own life because he can't stop drinking. I received an email exactly like that during the program on this topic. He wrote, "Please help me."

I am so thankful that we were able to pray with that man and give him the hope of the gospel. What I told him applies to anyone struggling to break free from alcohol and that is this: The Lord Jesus Christ is standing there with an outstretched hand, and He is desiring to break every bondage and save your soul from an eternal hell and give you life, and life more abundantly. Jesus Christ can and will set you free.

THE ROOT PROBLEM IS SIN

You see, alcoholism is only a symptom; sin is the root of the problem. So while this ministry may be viewed as judgmental because we preach a message of consecration, we will continue to do so because the only answer to the sin of alcoholism is found in the Cross of Jesus Christ.

I have never taken a drink of wine or any alcohol, so I can't speak of its so-called benefits. But all of us have seen or read in the news about alcohol's effect on other people — how it makes them act and what it can make them do. For some, their personalities completely change when they get a little drink under their belts, so to speak. People who drink lose their dignity and start acting foolish and silly. Others turn mean and violent, capable of doing untold harm to their families or themselves.

Police reports show that alcohol use is a direct contributor to reported cases of domestic violence and child abuse. So I fail to see why people, especially Christians, would want to defend the use of alcohol in any amount.

HEALTH BENEFIT OR EXCUSE?

Still, there are plenty of doctors and even preachers who defend the use of alcohol, saying there is nothing wrong with drinking in moderation. We have pastors preaching today that social drinking is acceptable and, sadly, some drink themselves. Remember: So goes the church, so goes the nation.

Actually, the main health benefit that doctors associate with red wine — resveratrol — is really found in the grape and not in the alcohol itself. If you want the benefit of the grape, drink grape juice or eat grapes. To say that you are drinking alcohol for health reasons is simply an excuse to sin.

In fact, there are actually many health risks to drinking alcohol. Why do you think they ask you if you drink alcohol when you apply for health insurance? It's because there is actually greater risk for adverse effects to your health than there are benefits.

As Brother Carl Brown pointed out on *Frances & Friends*, "Christians who don't really want to consecrate to the Lord are the ones who take up issues such as social drinking," and he is absolutely correct.

LOSS OF POWER

Quite simply put, drinking alcohol appeals to the flesh, not to the Spirit. The Holy Spirit will never lead one to drink alcohol. Churches defending alcohol use may as well have a big red neon sign blinking for everybody to see that says, "We've lost the power of God, and we're having to imitate." In other words, "We've got to put something in to take the place of the moving and operation of the Holy Spirit."

Ladies and gentlemen, be assured that there is absolutely nothing else that compares to the anointing and the power of the Holy Spirit in our personal lives and in the church of the Lord Jesus Christ.

"For these are not drunken, as you suppose, seeing it is but the third hour of the day. But this is that which was spoken by the prophet Joel; And it shall come to pass in the last days, saith God, I will pour out of My Spirit upon all flesh" (Acts 2:15-17).

As believers, the Lord gives us the power to live a consecrated life, and He reminds us in I Corinthians 6:19 that the *"body is the temple of the Holy Spirit."*

PLAYING WITH FIRE

Something in man always thinks he can control sin. Something in him says, "Oh, I can handle this; I can stop at one drink," but when you play around with sin, you are actually dealing with the spiritual realm. And, believe me, no mortal man is stronger than the spiritual powers of darkness. You are playing with fire. This is what you call deception! It's deception to think you can drink moderately and it has no effect on you. You are deceived. What if a problem arises in your life? You may turn to the alcohol when you never thought you would have before. You are tempting yourself and God to try to drink moderately: *"You shall not tempt the Lord your God"* (Mat. 4:7).

Even if you do not become an alcoholic, drinking alcohol can affect you spiritually in other ways. It is more than a coincidence that alcohol is referred to as "spirits."

DECEPTION

Alcohol, like any other drug, actually opens your mind to the spirit world. Satan has more leeway to plant suggestions in your mind that are anti-biblical when you use drugs. It's a well-known fact that other religions purposely use drugs in order to get in touch with their gods or spirits, which we as believers know are nothing more than demon spirits.

People often hallucinate after drinking, particularly after a tragic event or a stressful time in their lives. These hallucinations are demonic in nature. They often appear as "familiar spirits." The Bible says that the last days will be marked by pharmakeia (sorcery, drugs): *"For by your sorceries were all nations deceived"* (Rev. 18:23).

So, maybe you will not become the next alcoholic, but you may engage in some other sin. Many end up in fornication or homosexuality because they have opened themselves up to spirits of lust through alcohol and drug use. Many become angry and even commit murder under the influence of drugs. Many begin to believe false doctrine and fall away from truth in some way. You may leave the Message of the Cross.

You see, if you give your mind over to Satan often enough, or if you yield your mind to spirits rather than the Holy Spirit often enough, you will have no control over what lies you start to believe.

BE VIGILANT

The Bible says, *"Be sober, be vigilant; because your adversary the Devil, as a roaring lion, walks about, seeking whom he may devour"* (I Pet. 5:8).

When people are given over to false doctrine, it's actually a sign of God's judgment. I don't find it a coincidence that both false doctrine and the acceptance of alcohol are on the rise in our churches. The two go hand in hand.

Really, any believer should be convicted of drinking alcohol, but many have pushed away the conviction and chosen not to obey. The Holy Spirit will never lead you astray, but He does not force us to obey Him either. If we push Him away, He will not override our will or force us to repent.

"Neither repented they of their murders, nor of their sorceries, nor of their fornication, nor of their thefts" (Rev 9:21).

This is why it's so important for believers to develop a close personal relationship with the Lord and be Spirit-led.

He will show you right from wrong, but you must draw near to Him. The more you allow Him to be Lord of your life, the more that answers to moral questions such as these become very simple. It's our own thinking and intellect that get in the way. It's our intellect that devises excuses or tries to justify our sins. Look to the Lord for your answers.

AND
SARAH
SAW

A MIXED MESSAGE ON
MODERATE DRINKING

A MIXED MESSAGE ON MODERATE DRINKING

TWO EMAILS WERE WRITTEN to me in response to our discussions of alcohol on *Frances & Friends*. Here is the first email from Georgia:

> I wanted to contact you to tell you that I appreciate your program so much, and my husband and I are dependent on it and Jimmy Swaggart's sermons throughout the week. My husband and I recently were 'moderate' drinkers before watching your program this past month or so. Please don't assume we were defensive of alcohol to begin with; we simply were never exposed to any other way. We are in our early 20s, are newlyweds, university students, and we are learning to live as the Lord wants us to.

> Unfortunately, my husband was raised in a home where both his guardians are undoubtedly alcoholics. However, they defensively claim to drink 'socially' or 'moderately' even though they drink nearly every night, they also profess to be Christians and are very involved in their church. I grew up in a home in which the teachings of the Lord were completely foreign and blasphemed. I was

emotionally, physically, verbally, and sexually abused during my childhood. Alcohol, I know very well, influenced how I was treated and was raised. Alcohol is not a foreign notion to either of us, and because neither of us were raised in a home that believed in conviction, we just assumed there was nothing wrong with it.

My parents have always led me to believe that I deserved the way that I was treated, so I never bothered to evaluate the consequences of the consumption involved in my abuse. I wanted to point out, that drunkenness is a sin. No one can call in and argue with you about that. If the Lord meant for moderate drinking to be acceptable, that would mean it would be a moderate sin, and there is no such thing.

I study history and criminal justice. I would implore those who defend alcohol to look up for themselves the percentage of crime in this country that involves either the abuse of drugs or the consumption of alcohol, and even more so, the type of crime that occurs, for it is rarely a victimless crime. I am especially thankful for your program due to the discernment the Lord has revealed to me through it.

In America today, what is right and wrong is no longer black and white, but instead has been manipulated over the years into a large gray area. If children are raised to pick and choose from the Lord's instruction what to enforce into their lives, they will eventually grow numb to the Holy Spirit's convictions. This is so dangerous. If a 'Christian' parent believes in moderate drinking, either because they fail to look up what wine means for themselves or they simply denounce it so that they may choose their own preferences over the Lord's instruction, they are teaching their children not only to be lukewarm, but that that lifestyle is acceptable.

Shortly after we received the above email, we received another one dealing with the issue of moderate drinking (or drinking in moderation), which is really what we are dealing with (more so than drunkenness or alcoholism).

As the first email already mentioned, no one really argues that drunkenness is a sin. The disagreements, as well as lack of understanding, conviction, and repentance usually come concerning social or moderate drinking.

Both emails make very important observations and points concerning this issue. There are many pastors and believers still out there who do not agree with moderate drinking and are still convicted of it, even in these last days, even in this late hour. I've even heard of new believers who were convicted to leave their jobs after coming to Christ because their jobs involved the distribution of alcohol. They were not even consuming the alcohol, just distributing it. Ladies and gentlemen, we are far from being the only ones against the drinking of alcohol.

Here is the second email:

How ignorant is this so-called pastor that just called? 'Everything in moderation?' So, according to him, we can kill a moderate amount of people, steal moderately, lie a moderate amount, take cocaine moderately, and take poison in moderation too? Wow! This guy is teaching people? Run, flock, run! I wrote you a previous breakdown on the Greek word *wine*, used for three different types of 'juice of the grape or vine,' which you might not have. There were three types of 'juice of the grape or vine.'

1. Mixed with water (to stretch for the poor) like Kool-Aid
2. Old wine (turned to vinegar for vegetables and herbs)
3. Strong drink (fermented grape juice, made by adding some form of sweetener, sugar, etc.) to produce what we call wine, (one definition in English), containing alcohol.

All alcohol is poisonous to the human body in one way or another. It causes the brain to lose logic, bleed, and to blackout or die. Alcohol also poisons the whole body — stomach, bloodstream, kidney, bladder, etc. It also removes collagen from the skin, causing wrinkles and aging skin. This is why animals will usually stay clear of it — a lot smarter than humans? It is now the number one killer in the United States, and possibly the world now.

This pastor is really scary! He never studied as thoroughly as he said, or he would have known this. Christ never could have drank poisonous wine, or made it for others. He was without sin! He produced the best 'wine' (perfect whole grape juice for the wedding, as this was very hard and costly to get without the heat turning it to vinegar. Remember there was no refrigeration other than water, or underground storage. Strong drink actually would be easier to get, because of the heat there, this is why the guests were so shocked, like I am about a man in the pulpit teaching wrong interpretations of the Word. Your husband did a sermon on this in one of his crusades in the 1960s. The translation into English used the word *wine*, which had only one meaning in English, 'fermented hard drink.' A confusion in translation resulted.

WINE IN THE BIBLE

Let's continue to dig into how wine was used in the Bible and during ancient times. Keeping in mind that the Greek word for wine is *oinos*, let's look at what Dr. Spiros Zodhiates said in the *Lexical Aids To The New Testament*.

Zodhiates said:

Wine derived from grapes. The mention of the bursting of the wine skins in Matthew 9:17; Mark 2:22; and, Luke 5:37 implies fermentation (see Eph. 5:18; cf. Jn. 2:10; I Tim. 3:8; and, Titus 2:3). From the intoxicating effects of wine and the idolatrous use of it among the heathen, wine signifies communion in the intoxicating idolatries of the mystic Babylon (Rev. 14:8; cf. Jer. 51:7).

From Jewish custom of giving a cup of medicated wine to condemned criminals just before their execution to dull their senses, it figuratively denotes the dreadful judgments of God upon sinners (Rev. 14:10, 16:19; cf. Is. 51:17, 21, 23; Jer. 25:15). The drinking of wine could be a stumbling block and Paul enjoins abstinence in this respect, as in others, so as to avoid giving an occasion of stumbling to a brother (Rom. 14:21). Contrast I Timothy 5:23, which has an entirely different connection (cf. the word gleukos [1098], sweet new wine, and sikera [4608], strong drink).

In this same reference, we find the meaning of the word *sikera.* Zodhiates continues, "Strong drink, and intoxicating liquor, whether wine (Num. 28:7), or more usually, that which is prepared from grain, fruit, honey, dates, as in Luke 1:15 where it occurs together with oinos (3631), wine. See Leviticus 10:9; Deuteronomy 29:6; Judges 13:4, 7, 14."

In *The Words & Works of Jesus Christ,* by J. Dwight Pentecost, he quotes J. W. Shepard as saying: "Jesus made real wine out of water. But there was a great difference between the Palestinian wine of that time and the alcoholic mixtures which today go under the name of wine. Their simple vintage was taken with three parts of water and would correspond more or less to our grape juice. It would be worse than blasphemy to suppose, because Jesus made wine, that He justifies the drinking usages of modern society with its bars, strong drinks, and resulting evils."

It is necessary to understand the use of wine in the New Testament. In his article, "Wine-Drinking in New Testament Times," Robert H. Stein says: "In ancient times wine was usually stored in large pointed jugs called amphorae. When wine was to be used, it was poured from the amphorae into large bowls called kraters, where it was mixed with water. From these kraters, cups, or kylix, were then filled. What is important for us to note is that before wine was drunk, it was mixed with water. The kylix was not filled from the amphorae but from the kraters."

Wine was always mixed with water, both to help purify the water of that day and also to prevent intoxication. So, often when the Bible spoke of wine, it was basically speaking of purified water. The ratio of water to wine varied. Homer (Odyssey IX, 208f.) mentions a ratio of 20-to-1, 20 parts water to one part wine.

In *Bible Wines* by William Patton, we learn that Hippocrates also considered, "Twenty parts of water to one part of the Thracian wine to be the proper beverage." Pliny (Natural History XIV, vi, 54) mentions a ratio of eight parts water to one part wine.

In another ancient work, *Banquet of the Learned of Athenaeus,* which was written around A.D. 200, we find, in Book Ten, a collection of statements from earlier writers about drinking practices. A quotation from a play by Aristophanes said, "The ration of water to wine is 3-to-1." Sometimes the ratio does go down 1-to-1 (and even lower), but when the mixture gets this low, it is referred to as "strong drink," which was completely unacceptable. Drinking wine unmixed, such as this, was looked upon as a "Scythian" or barbarian custom.

Solomon wrote, *"Wine is a mocker, strong drink is raging"* (Prov. 20:1).

Proverbs 31:4-5 says, *"It is not for kings ... To drink wine, nor for princes strong drink: Lest they drink, and forget the law, and pervert the judgment of any of the afflicted,"* pointing out the use of alcohol is especially forbidden for those who would be leaders.

A MIXED BEVERAGE

It is evident that wine was seen in ancient times as a beverage. Yet, as a beverage, it was always thought of as a mixed drink. Plutarch (Sumposiacs III, ix), for instance, states, "We call a mixture 'wine,' although the larger of the component parts is water."

The ratio of water might vary, but only barbarians drank it unmixed. And, a mixture of wine and water of equal parts was seen as a "strong drink" and frowned upon. The term *wine* or *oinos* in the ancient world, then, did not mean wine as we understand it today, but rather wine mixed with water, and sometimes just simply grape juice.

Usually writers simply referred to the mixture of water and wine as "wine." To indicate that the beverage was not a mixture of water and wine, he would say "unmixed (akratesteron) wine."

Some even suggest that Timothy was so concerned with separating himself from those who used wine improperly that he had stopped mixing wine in his water altogether and caused himself stomach problems (I Tim. 5:23).

Again, the water of that day needed the wine for purification. It could be boiled, but that was difficult to do in those days. It could be filtered, but that wasn't really a safe method. So, it was easiest to add a little wine to kill the germs. Today, we do not need to add wine at all. We have other things for purification, as well as for medicines.

Clearly what people drink today and call moderate, the Bible and cultures of ancient times (including even many pagan cultures) would have considered a wrongful, and even barbaric, use of wine. It's amazing that with all of our increased knowledge in modern times, our consciences have been so dulled. We, as a people, have become quite good at rationalizing whatever it is we want to do, while we have become terribly inept at sensing the convictions of the Holy Spirit.

And, of course, our insensitivities include much more than just alcohol use. As well, false teachers make it even easier to ignore our convictions as they tell us what our flesh wants to hear and help us dismiss what the Lord is speaking to our hearts.

"Having their conscience seared with a hot iron" (I Tim. 4:2).

As the above emails pointed out, "There is no such thing as moderate sin." God, help us to hear Your heart on this subject instead of our fleshly desires! And, make no mistake; it is always our flesh and never the Holy Spirit that draws us to want to drink alcohol.

ABSTINENCE

We believe the Bible teaches total and complete abstinence at all times from any and all kinds of alcoholic beverages. Just as in Bible times, there is presently that which is holy and that which is unholy. As ought to be overly obvious, alcohol falls into the category of the unholy and the unclean.

The main Hebrew and Greek word for wine, *oinos,* can mean either unfermented grape juice or intoxicating wine. The English word for wine originally had two meanings also — unfermented juice or alcoholic drink.

In the Bible, anytime there are verses showing God's approval of drinking wine, it is speaking of the unfermented grape juice. Verses that expose the evils of wine are speaking about intoxicating wine or alcohol. The Bible says all alcoholic drink is evil. It is not just the amount one drinks that makes drinking a sin.

God condemns the drinking itself: *"Wine is a mocker, strong drink is raging: and whosoever is deceived thereby is not wise"* (Prov. 20:1).

God does not lead us into evil; He delivers us from it. He does not teach us to practice evil in moderation either. Jesus did not make, use, approve, commend, or tell us to use intoxicating wine. God made man to have fellowship with Him, but alcohol goes directly to the brain, which is the communication center of the body. Alcohol, thereby, interferes with God's purpose for mankind and our relationship with Him.

AND SARAH SAW

MORE THAN ONE
WAY TO GOD?

MORE THAN ONE WAY TO GOD?

FOR GOD SO LOVED the world, that He gave His only begotten Son, that whosoever believes in Him should not perish, but have everlasting life (Jn. 3:16).

God's Word tells us that without the shedding of blood, there is no remission of sin (Heb. 9:22). Fallen humanity's only choice then is to find blood that is pure, untainted by sin, and, thereby, able to take our place in death. Thank the Lord — that blood has been provided!

We must ever let it be known that it was the Lord Jesus Christ who was the only One worthy and the only One whose blood can wash clean the souls of men! Death was the price for sin, and it was Jesus, hallelujah, who paid this price and died in the place of those who would come to Him.

"For the wages of sin is death; but the gift of God is eternal life through Jesus Christ our Lord" (Rom. 6:23).

Jesus is without question the one and only way to God.

Revelation 13:8 says that Jesus was the Lamb slain from the foundation of the world. None can be rescued from hell who refuse the blood of God's only Son.

CHRIST ALONE!

The reason human beings experience a sense of distance or disconnect with God is because of our sin. God's holiness prevents Him from fellowshipping with unrighteousness.

You see, man cannot save himself because all men have inherited a sin nature. Neither can one man die for another. Not even the death of an innocent animal is enough. In the Old Testament, the Lord instituted the animal sacrifices, but this only served as a temporary covering for sin until Christ would completely take sin away.

"For it is not possible that the blood of bulls and of goats should take away sins" (Heb 10:4).

Yet, even in this temporary situation, God always only had one specific place, one tabernacle, or one brazen altar in which He would accept the sacrifices. His conditions were designed to typify the sacrifice of Christ, which was to come. Some depraved individuals throughout history even tried sacrificing babies upon evil heathen altars in a desperate attempt to atone for sin.

However, Christ alone was spotless, making Him the only suitable sacrifice for our sin. Eternal life and salvation are only available to those who identify with His substitutionary death at Calvary.

"Therefore we are buried with Him by baptism into death: that like as Christ was raised up from the dead by the glory of the Father, even so we also should walk in newness of life" (Rom. 6:4).

JESUS — THE ONLY WAY TO GOD

Tragically, however, in both the church and the world today, we have many who are teaching that there is more than one way to God.

These say that as long as you sincerely pursue goodness in your life and follow your conscience to the best of your ability, whatever path you take will ultimately lead you to God and bring you to heaven one day. These individuals could make no greater mistake! With all our creature comforts, entertainments, and distractions, it may be hard in this modern age to comprehend the dire consequences of sin.

Yet, it is the actual reason our physical bodies die, and spiritually-speaking, we are already "... *dead in trespasses and sins*" (Eph. 2:1).

However, unlike the Jews, we do not have to watch the fires consume the flesh of the animal sacrifices, nor do we have to physically apply the blood of an innocent lamb across the doorposts of our homes to escape an angel of death like the Jews did in Egypt (Ex., Chpt. 12).

As well, we did not see God strike dead the priests who offered up *"strange fire"* to Him (Lev. 10:1-2), meaning that their offering failed to typify Christ's sacrifice. The Lord allowed such vivid events, however, to try to show man the spiritual magnitude that Christ's death on the Cross would be. It was, in fact, the only way God could have ever reached us.

A DANGEROUS DIRECTION

Sadly, one of the most outspoken proponents that Jesus is not the only way to God is Oprah Winfrey. Although raised Baptist, she has come to embrace an entirely different and dangerous spirituality. This is not only sad for the sake of Oprah's soul, but also for the souls of the many she is now leading astray.

Several years ago on her own program, Oprah emphatically stated, "There couldn't possibly be just one way!" Here is the resulting dialogue when a woman in the audience reminded her of Jesus.

Oprah (speaking to the woman in the audience): Do you think that if you are somewhere on the planet, and you never hear the name of Jesus, but yet, you live with a loving heart, you lived as Jesus would have had you to live, you lived for the same purpose that Jesus came to the planet to teach us all, but you are in some remote part of the earth, and you never heard the name of Jesus, you cannot get to heaven, you think?

Woman: God knows the heart.

Oprah: Does God care about your heart, or does God care whether you call His Son Jesus?"

Woman: Jesus cannot come back until that gospel is preached in the four corners of this earth, so, you know, figure it out.

Oprah: Okay, I can't get into a religious argument with you.

What a sarcastic statement with which Oprah ends this conversation, as if she had not been having a religious discussion all along!

WITHOUT EXCUSE

Thank God, we still have a few brave Christians in this world. I'm sure this lady in the audience had no idea how far-reaching her defense of Jesus would be that day. And though this lady was right in that the gospel will be preached to the four corners of the earth, according to Scripture, it is also true that even if someone does not hear the name of Jesus, he will still stand before God without excuse.

"For the invisible things of Him from the creation of the world are clearly seen, being understood by the things that are made, even His eternal power and Godhead; so that they are without excuse" (Rom. 1:20).

"Behold, the former things are come to pass, and new things do I declare: before they spring forth I tell you of them" (Isa. 42:9).

God does not fail to make Himself known to us. This lady was also correct in that God knows our hearts. If the heart is truly seeking Him and is repentant of sin, then it is the job of the Holy Spirit to lead us to Christ and His Cross. The Holy Spirit, who is God, will never fail to lead us to Jesus.

"Howbeit when He, the Spirit of truth, is come, He will guide you into all truth: for He shall not speak of Him-self; but whatsoever He shall hear, that shall He speak:

and He will show you things to come. He shall glorify Me (Christ): for He shall receive of Mine, and shall show it unto you. All things that the Father has are Mine: therefore said I, that He shall take of Mine, and shall show it unto you" (Jn. 16:13-15).

Christians should never apologize for their faith in the glorious gospel of our Lord. God is just, and He will always do what is fair and right in the life of every person on the planet.

DIFFERENT ROUTES?

In a 2004 ABC News interview with Charles Gibson, President George Bush responded to the question of whether or not Christians and Muslims worship the same God.

He said, "I think we do. We have different routes of getting to the Almighty.... But I want you to understand, I want your listeners to understand, I don't get to decide who goes to heaven. The almighty God decides who goes to heaven, and I am on my personal walk."

President Bush, who has professed to be a born-again Christian, also made this heretical statement in an interview on Al Arabiya television: "I believe in an almighty God, and I believe that all the world, whether they be Muslim, Christian, or any other religion, prays to the same God ... I believe there is a universal God. I believe the God that the Muslim prays to is the same God that I pray to. After all, we all came from Abraham. I believe in that universality."

Let's now look right within the professing Christian church itself. Here is a 1998 television dialogue between Billy Graham and Robert Schuller as reported in the May-June 1997 *Foundation* magazine:

Schuller: Tell me, what do you think is the future of Christianity?

Graham: Well, Christianity and being a true believer, you know, I think there's the body of Christ which comes from all the Christian groups around the world or outside the Christian groups. I think everybody that loves Christ, or knows Christ, whether they're conscious of it or not, they're members of the body of Christ ... and that's what God is doing today, He's calling people out of the world for His name, whether they come from the Muslim world, or the Buddhist world, or the Christian world, or the non-believing world, they are members of the body of Christ because they've been called by God. They may not even know the name of Jesus, but they know in their hearts that they need something that they don't have, and they turn to the only light that they have, and I think that they are saved, and that they're going to be with us in heaven.

Schuller: Well, what I hear you saying, that it's possible for Jesus Christ to come into human hearts and soul and life, even if they've been born in darkness and have never had exposure to the Bible. Is that a correct interpretation of what you're saying?

Graham: Yes, it is, because I believe that. I've met people in various parts of the world in tribal situations, that they have never seen a Bible or heard about a Bible, and never heard of Jesus, but they've believed in their hearts that there was a God, and they've tried to live a life that was quite apart from the surrounding community in which they lived.

Schuller: This is fantastic! I'm so thrilled to hear you say that! There's a wideness in God's mercy!
Graham: There is. There definitely is.

Actually, the Roman Catholic universal catechism says almost exactly the same thing: "Those who, through no fault of their own, do not know the gospel of Christ or his Church, but who nevertheless seek God with a sincere heart and, moved by grace, try in their actions to do his will as they know it through the dictates of their conscience, those too may achieve eternal salvation."

This is also very similar to Oprah's response to the woman in her audience that if a person tries to be good, sincere, and loving, he can make it to heaven without Christ. But again, no amount of good works can atone for sin. It took the death of a perfect sacrifice.

In a June 16, 2005, CNN interview with Larry King, Billy Graham made these statements:

King: But what about those faiths — the Mormons and the others that you mentioned — [they] believe in Christ. They believe they will meet Christ. What about those like the Jews, the Muslims, who don't believe they …"

Graham: That's in God's hands. I can't be the judge.

King: You don't judge them?
Graham: No.

King: How do you feel …
Graham: … going to hell and all that.

King: How do you feel when you see a lot of these strong Christian leaders go on television and say, 'You are condemned, you will live in hell if you do not accept Jesus Christ,' and they are forceful and judgmental?
Graham: Well, they have a right to say that, and they are true to a certain extent, but I don't — that's not my calling. My calling is to preach the love of God and the forgiveness of God and the fact that He does forgive us. That's what the Cross is all about, what the resurrection is all about, that's the gospel. And you can get off on all kinds of different side trends, and in my earlier ministry, I did the same, but as I got older, I guess I became more mellow and more forgiving and more loving."

ONE NAME ONLY!

This is quite shocking because the Bible makes it completely clear that salvation comes by one name only.

Matthew 7:14: *"Because strait is the gate, and narrow is the way, which leads unto life, and few there be that find it."*

Acts 4:12: *"Neither is there salvation in any other: for there is none other name under heaven given among men, whereby we must be saved."*

In Acts 16:30-31, a prison guard asks Paul and Silas this question when he sees that the power of God had broken their prison bands: *"... Sirs, what must I do to be saved? And they said, Believe on the Lord Jesus Christ, and you shall be saved, and your house."*

The list of Scriptures goes on and on:

I John 5:12: *"He who has the Son has life; and he who has not the Son of God has not life."*

John 14:6: *"Jesus said unto him, I am the way, the truth, and the life: no man comes unto the Father, but by Me."*

Jn. 10:7-9: *"Then said Jesus unto them again, Verily, verily, I say unto you, I am the door of the sheep. All who ever came before Me are thieves and robbers: but the sheep did not hear them. I am the door: by Me if any man enter in, he shall be saved, and shall go in and out, and find pasture."*

We hope that these confusing statements made by Billy Graham in recent years are due to some of the medical complications he has experienced because in Graham's early ministry, he clearly preached that Jesus was the only way. However, we must warn those who would take his recent statements to heart and head down the path of apostasy as a result of their confidence in Graham.

SIN!

What so many of these leaders have done is avoid the subject of sin altogether or somehow redefine it so that the solution can be something other than Christ.

In *Self-Esteem, The New Reformation*, Robert Schuller wrote, "Salvation is defined as rescue from shame to glory. It is salvation from guilt to pride, from fear to love, from distrust to faith, from hypocrisy to honest ... so lack of trust or a lack of self-worth is the central core of sin."

Schuller's statement here sounds very similar to what Oprah described in Marianne Williamson's book, *A Return To Love*. She described how New Age guru, Williamson, spoke of salvation as choosing to move in the direction of love (light) rather than moving in the direction of fear (darkness).

Again, man cannot choose salvation through correct action; it took the blood of the Lamb. By completely dismissing their need for a Saviour, these leaders dismiss Jesus as the only way to God.

Lord, help us all to recognize our need for the saving blood of Jesus Christ.

AND SARAH SAW

CHAPTER 16

SPIRITS OF LIGHT

SPIRITS OF LIGHT

LEST SATAN SHOULD GET an advantage of us: for we are not ignorant of his devices (II Cor. 2:11).

Scripture has made it perfectly clear that the Devil masquerades as "light" and or an "angel of light." In Latin, the name *Lucifer* means "light-bearer."

II Corinthians 11:14 says, *"And no marvel; for Satan himself is transformed into an angel of light."*

Therefore, any experience with spiritual "light" must be thoroughly examined under the microscope of the one true light, the Word of God.

Light, it seems, has always been used as a metaphor for heightened, perhaps even spiritual, experiences or understandings. Often we hear people speak of being "enlightened." Some believed to possess spiritual empowerment have been called "illuminated."

Traditionally, even artists have depicted both religious and secular leaders, heroes, and great thinkers shining with brilliant light, perhaps even beneath a halo.

Now, the problem we encounter here is that such

inspiration is usually viewed in a positive manner. It is hard to call evil what we normally associate with good. Nevertheless, the Bible bids us to *"believe not every spirit, but try the spirits whether they are of God"* (I Jn. 4:1).

It seems that throughout history many have encountered spirits of light but failed to recognize their source. In fact, many who claim to have light believe they started with the best of intentions. They believed their search for light was search for truth.

For instance, Freemasons claim to be searching for light, hence, the symbolic use of the blindfold in many of their rituals. But, truth cannot be found outside of the Word of God.

An attempt to discover light or truth apart from it actually demonstrates a lack of faith in the truth. The Lord has made it clear that seeking truth means seeking Him. He alone is *the* Light.

"He reveals the deep and secret things: He knows what is in the darkness, and the light dwells with Him" (Dan. 2:22).

"But without faith it is impossible to please Him: for he who comes to God must believe that He is, and that He is a rewarder of them who diligently seek Him" (Heb. 11:6).

FALSE LIGHT

Many false prophets and cult leaders claim to have received revelation knowledge from angels of light, and usually these revelations became the foundation for their perilous societies.

Muhammad claimed that the angel Gabriel came to him. He explained that, "a luminous being grasped him by the throat and commanded him to repeat the sacred word."

Another angel of light named Moroni visited the founder of Mormonism, Joseph Smith, who was already a "romancer and diviner" (familiar with occult communication). Smith said his angel led him to a set of golden plates, which he translated from "reformed Egyptian" into English with the help of magic stones.

The final product was the Book of Mormon.

Sun Myung Moon, founder of the Unification Church, claims that Jesus appeared to him in a vision, asking Moon to complete the work He began. Clearly this "Jesus" was not the Jesus of the Bible. The real Jesus *finished* His work (Jn. 19:30).

The apostle Paul specifically warned us of such false messengers: *"But though we, or an angel form heaven, preach any other gospel unto you than that which we have preached unto you, let him be accursed"* (Gal. 1:8).

Remember, though, Satan's light does not necessarily have to appear in angelic form. Even the simplest sensation of enlightenment could have come from an ungodly source. Not surprisingly, then, light is a cornerstone of New Age teaching as well.

NEW AGERS

New Agers, in fact, refer to themselves as "light-workers."

Warren Smith, former New Ager and author of *Deceived on Purpose*, has described one particular experience he had with New Age light.

In his book, *The Light That Was Dark*, Smith explained what happened during one particular psychic reading: "It was toward the end of the reading that I first noticed the whirling sensation over my head. I tried to ignore it, but it wouldn't go away. It was a strange but not unpleasant feeling that seemed to flutter and vibrate and even tingle above me. I was startled when Bonnie picked up on it. 'Are you aware that there is a ball of light over your head? ... You are being shown that you have a lot of help on the other side.'"

A best-selling book of the 1990s, *Embraced by the Light* by Betty J. Eadie describes the good and loving feelings that often accompany mystical experiences with the "light."

It is also important to note that New Agers consider this light their source of life as well as their god, hence, their frequent usage of the term *God-light* or *life-light*.

New Age mystic Alice Bailey describes the light in this manner: "To this light the mystics testify, and it is this light into which they enter, and which enters into them, revealing the light which is laten and drawing it forth to potency ... This is the outstanding fact of scientific mysticism. God is light...."

On the slopes of Mount Shasta, California, Guy Ballard, leader of the "I Am" cult, encountered a spirit guide known as the ascended master, St. Germain. Ballard says this spirit mentor gave him a "liquid-light" to drink, explaining that the liquid was as pure as life itself, coming directly from the "universal supply."

ANOTHER JESUS

Neale Donald Walsch, New Age author of *Conversations with God*, describes his encounter with "God" as "some invisible force," which caused his hand to write on its own.

This phenomenon is actually an occult channeling practice known as "automatic handwriting," where one yields his mind to a demonic voice. Of course, Scripture completely forbids any such practice, but Walsch, unfortunately, did not heed the warning, thus, believing the voice he heard was God.

According to one source, "He was amazed when 'God' immediately answered his letter by speaking to him through an inner voice. That night, and in subsequent conversations, Walsch wrote down all of the dictated answers to his questions."

Even more disturbing is that one year after the events of Sept. 11, 2001, Walsch published another book, *The New Revelations*, which directly attacked the saving power of Jesus. Walsch's god put salvation into the hands of man.

"Walsch explained that 'God' was proposing a post-September 11 'PEACE Plan' that would help to bring the world's widely varying religions and belief systems closer together ... Walsch's 'god' warned: 'Yet let me make something clear. The era of the Single Saviour is over. What is needed now is joint action, combined effort, collective co-creation.'"

Marianne Williamson, another well-recognized New Ager largely promoted by Oprah Winfrey, wrote a book entitled *Reflections on Love*. Williamson's book was based on *A Course in Miracles* by Helen Schucman, an associate professor of medical psychology at Columbia University. Schucman had also experienced "god" through an inner voice, and this voice actually claimed to be Jesus!

Schucman began, "... receiving channeled messages from a speaker who would later identify himself as Jesus Christ. The messages began with the words, 'Please take notes,' this is not optional."

So Helen Schucman, an atheist Jewish psychologist, began writing and for the next 10 years, the voice is said to have dictated 'in an inaudible voice' over 500,000 words contained in the three volumes.

And apparently the "Jesus" of *The Course In Miracles* was not impressed with Christianity; in fact, it was his mission to change it completely: "The primary reason for the Course is the 'Correcting of the errors of Christianity ... To foster spiritual development through the study and practice of, *A Course In Miracles*, a set of three books channeled by Jesus ... to teach the Course's reinterpretation of traditional Christian principles such as sin, suffering, forgiveness, atonement, and the meaning of the crucifixion...'"

Another prominent New Age teacher, Barbara Marx Hubbard, experienced the light in an intense vision she said occurred while she was in a dreamlike state.

"... She could see the earth and its people were now

surrounded by a radiant light. She watched as the whole planet was 'aligned' in 'a magnetic field of love' and lifted up by the brilliant light. Widespread healings took place as individuals experienced the merging of their own 'inner light' with the bright light that was surrounding them. A tremendous force emanating from the light sent powerful currents of joyful energy 'rippling' through the body of humanity. The world celebrated as all the earth was born again."

And, unfortunately, Hubbard also came to believe that this light was Christ giving her an alternative to the Armageddon scenario found in biblical prophecy.

"... In 1979, she had a revelation that the presence in her 1966 vision had been 'Christ' ... Hubbard's 'Christ' teaches that the violent Armageddon script described in the Bible does not have to happen, that it is only a 'possible' future, emphasizing that a more 'positive' future can and will manifest when humanity — without exception — openly declares its 'oneness' with him and all creation."

This is an outright attack on Christianity; there is no alternative to God's Word. All of it has come to pass and will continue to come to pass.

"Think not that I am come to destroy the law, or the prophets: I am not come to destroy, but to fulfill. For verily I say unto you, Till heaven and earth pass, one jot or one tittle shall in no wise pass from the law, till all be fulfilled" (Mat. 5:17-18).

And furthermore, it is the antichrist who Daniel identifies as having a false plan of peace. *"He shall magnify himself in his heart, and by peace shall destroy many"* (Dan. 8:25).

NEW AGE LIGHT

These occult and completely anti-Christian dealings with New Age light are attacking the modern church from the inside as well. For instance, one particular form of so-called Christian counseling developed by Dr. Ed Smith is termed *theophostic* counseling or *theophostic* prayer ministry.

Smith created the word *theophostic* from two Greek words: *theos* meaning "God" and *phos* meaning "light." Similar to the psychological models of "inner healing," theophostic counseling claims to heal one of harmful memories by bringing "light" directly into the memory.

Another pastor bringing New Age light into the church (and whose writings have been endorsed by Rick Warren) is Leonard Sweet. He has stated, "A surprisingly central feature of all the world's religions is the language of light in communicating the divine and symbolizing the union of the human with the divine: Muhammad's light-filled cave, Moses' burning bush, Paul's blinding light, Fox's 'inner light,' Krishna's Lord of Light, Bohme's light-filled cobbler shop, Plotinus' fire experiences, Bodhisattvas with the flow of Kundalini's fire erupting from their fontanelles, and so on."

He also acknowledges New Agers for helping him find the "new light," which he actually believes to have enhanced his Christianity: "I have followed those 'New Light leaders' ...

[Some] of those who led [me] into new light are: ... Matthew Fox, Richard Mouw, Rowan Williams...."

In *The Destiny of the Nations,* Alice Bailey even defined the New Age concept of Christmas:

> Spiritually the Christmas season is about the light, the promise of the Divine, and the birth of the Christ Consciousness in the human heart inaugurating an era of right human relations. This energy remains ever with us, 'The Christ in you, the hope of glory' ... During the 2000 years since Pisces has seen the spreading of light. Aquarius will see the rising of the light with Christ as the eternal symbol of both these great impulses. Humanity will move from the birth stages of the light within to the lifting of the life light in sacrifice, as we become the Risen Ones.

A FALSE BIBLE

The New Age "Bible," *The Message* (which some refer to as "The Mess"), has also taken every opportunity to distort any biblical reference to light, rewording it to fit New Age doctrines. We will not attempt to print all the Scriptures from *The Message* pertaining to this, but here are a couple of examples:

Psalms 8:5:

The King James Version of the Bible: *"For Thou hast made him a little lower than the angels, and hast crowned him with glory and honour."*

The Message: "Yet we've so narrowly missed being gods, bright with Eden's dawn light."

Psalms 27:1:

The King James Version of the Bible: *"The LORD is my light and salvation; whom shall I fear? The LORD is the strength of my life; of whom shall I be afraid?"*

The Message: "Light, space, zest — that's God. So, with him on my side I'm fearless, afraid of no one and nothing."

It is important to note, as well, that many pagan religions worship a sun god and believe his rays of light to be the life-giving source for the earth and its inhabitants. The ancient Babylonian sun god cult has actually infiltrated nearly all false religions to this day. Islam has an interesting twist to this story. Allah, the god of Islam, is said to be the moon god who was married to the sun goddess. The symbol of the crescent moon is prominent in the Muslim culture.

Acts 2:28

The King James Version of the Bible: *"Thou has made known to me the ways of life; Thou shalt make me full of joy with Thy countenance."*

The Message: "You've got my feet on the life-path, with your face shining sun-joy all around."

Acts 26:23

The King James Version of the Bible: *"That Christ should suffer, and that He should be the first that should rise from the dead, and should shew light unto the people, and to the Gentiles."*

The Message: One, the Messiah must die; two, raised from the dead, he would be the first rays of God's daylight shining on people far and near, people both godless and God-fearing.

In the next examples, we see the use of the term *golden circle*. Circles have always been an integral part of the paganism and witchcraft and, thus, the New Age as well.

The circle has been used as a symbol of the universe, to enforce the appearance of demons, and to symbolize phallic sun-god worship in freemasonry.

Also, rather than making Christ the head as the Bible teaches, the New Age tends to refer to Him as the center of something, like a circle.

Revelation 2:1

The King James Version of the Bible: *"Unto the angel of the church of Ephesus write, These things saith He that holdeth the seven stars in His right hand, who walketh in the midst of the seven golden candlesticks."*

The Message: "Write this to Ephesus, to the angel of the church. The One with seven stars in his right-fist grip, striding through the golden seven-lights' circle, speaks."

Revelation 2:5

The King James Version of the Bible: *"Remember therefore from whence thou art fallen, and repent, and do the first works; or else I will come unto thee quickly, and will remove thy candlestick out of its place, except thou repent."*

The Message: "Do you have any idea how far you've

fallen? A Lucifer fall! Turn back! Recover your dear early love. No time to waste, for I'm well on my way to removing your light from the golden circle."

Ladies and gentlemen, let me close this chapter with the words of the Lord Jesus Christ recorded in John 8:12: *"I am the light of the world: he that followeth Me shall not walk in darkness, but shall have the light of life."*

AND SARAH SAW

CHAPTER 17

HE OPENED TO US
THE SCRIPTURES

HE OPENED TO US THE SCRIPTURES

ONE OF THE MOST frequent questions we receive on *Frances & Friends* has to do with Bible translations — their accuracy, credibility, and their use by preachers in the local church.

The translation (as it is known) that seems to stir the most controversy is *The Message*, which is neither a Bible nor a translation.

Yet for more than 13 years, modern churches embracing a feel-good-about-yourself doctrine have been encouraging their congregations to trade in the Word of God for a book about the Bible that reads like a secular novel.

The reason this thought-for-thought interpretation is so popular is because many Christians know so little of the Bible that it's hard for them to discern if what they are hearing from the pulpit is, in fact, Scripture.

That's what makes a book like *The Message* so dangerous to the saved and to the unsaved. It may have a biblical sound, but it is not the Bible. It was written by an educated man, but it was not inspired by the Holy Spirit.

ABOUT THE AUTHOR

The Message: The Bible In Contemporary Language is one of more than 30 books written by Eugene Peterson — a retired Presbyterian minister and former professor of spiritual theology.

As a lover of storytelling, Peterson often quotes and references writers of fiction in his own books and sermons.

In 2007 at a writers symposium, Peterson gave a rare interview to Dr. Dean Nelson, the founder and director of the journalism program at Point Loma Nazarene.

Nelson questioned the influence and quotations by fiction writers in Peterson's work, including authors Wendell Berry, Flannery O'Connor, Walker Percy, Wallace Stegner, Fyodor Dostoyevsky, Anne Tyler, and James Joyce.

In response to Nelson's interview question, Peterson said that as a young pastor, he experienced an "imagination conversion" while reading *Ulysses* — a famously modernist novel by James Joyce — which revealed to him a clear comparison between the ordinary individuals in his congregation and the fictional book's main character.

"I find fiction writers some of the best spiritual writers whether they are Christians or not, religious or not, they're probing the ordinary world of our lives," Peterson said. "They're great. I think pastors should read fiction a lot more than they do."

This is concerning since fiction is defined as written stories about people and events that are not real and literature that tells stories that are imagined by the writer.

Peterson thinks so highly of imagination and fiction that he confirmed to Nelson his belief that all seminary students should spend their first two years in literature training.

This point about Peterson's love of storytelling and fiction is important because a storyteller's main goal is to captivate and entertain an audience, not necessarily relay a truth to them.

It was reaction from his audience — his congregation — that led Peterson to write *The Message*. The book's publisher, NavPress, quotes Peterson's reason for the project: "While I was teaching a class on Galatians, I began to realize that the adults in my class weren't feeling the vitality and directness that I sensed as I read and studied the New Testament in its original Greek…. I hoped to bring the New Testament to life for two different types of people: those who hadn't read the Bible because it seemed too distant and irrelevant and those who had read the Bible so much that it had become 'old hat.'"

So Peterson rewrote his own version of Galatians, shared it with his congregation, and later included portions of it in another one of his other books, *Traveling Light*, which was read by a NavPress editor.

The editor liked what he read and asked Peterson if he would be interested in "translating" the entire New Testament. Peterson left his pastorate and started writing full-time.

Ladies and gentlemen, I point this out because this is how book deals are made.

Editors and publishers know what books will sell, and

they know how to market them; that's their business.

It's the publisher who called *The Message* a "version of the Bible," not Peterson, although he does not argue the point.

In an interview with *Christianity Today*, Peterson said, "When I'm in a congregation where somebody uses [*The Message*] in the Scripture reading, it makes me a little uneasy. I would never recommend it be used as saying, 'Hear the Word of God from *The Message*.' But it surprises me how many do."

Unfortunately, with the endorsement of high-profile ministers, authors, secular and Christian rock stars, and politicians, *The Message* has been marketed and pushed onto pulpits and into the hands of pastors who are willing to compromise and into the ears of undiscerning Christians. It's concerning that 10 million copies of this book have been sold.

As Carl Brown pointed out on *Frances & Friends*: "Professing Christians have no desire for the Word of God, and that's a problem because if you don't know what the Bible says, then anything goes, and that's what we see happening in this country — there lies that vacuum because preachers are not preaching the Word of God to people, and preachers who do that are going to give a heavy account."

WORDS IN *THE MESSAGE*

According to its publisher, *The Message* is a "reading Bible" written in the same type of conversational language that we use to speak with friends.

It's been stripped of "formal terms" (i.e., Lord Jesus) and verse numbers to make it read like "one of your favorite novels."

In reality, *The Message* includes disrespectful, New Age, occult-related, and racy street language.

How can these types of words bless, encourage, and strengthen the child of God whose mind has been regenerated by the Holy Spirit?

NO COMPARISON

The comparison of the Lord's Prayer between the King James Version of the Bible and *The Message* book should be enough to make any Christian shudder:

> *The Message*:
> Our Father in heaven,
> Reveal who you are.
> Set the world right;
> Do what's best —
> as above, so below.
> Keep us alive with three square meals.
> Keep us forgiven with you
> and forgiving others.
> Keep us safe from ourselves and the Devil.
> You're in charge!
> You can do anything you want!
> You're ablaze in beauty!
> Yes. Yes. Yes.

The King James Version of the Bible:
Our Father which art in heaven,
Hallowed be thy name.
Thy kingdom come.
Thy will be done in earth,
as it is in heaven.
Give us this day our daily bread.
And forgive us our debts,
as we forgive our debtors.
And lead us not into temptation,
but deliver us from evil:
For Thine is the kingdom,
and the power, and the glory, for ever.
Amen.

With the cut of just four words — *"Hallowed be Thy name"* — Peterson removed the believer's acknowledgment of God's holiness and reverence for His name.

With the addition of four words — "as above, so below" — Peterson replaced God's all-important will being done with a well-known occult term.

The author of *The Message* decided that the curse word *damn* should be used frequently as well as these crude and sexually explicit terms throughout his book: Scent of sex, sex orgies, slut, spreading your legs, and hell-raisers.

These are words used by secular novelists, not by someone inspired by the Spirit of the living God.

Much more could be said about this book that is

believed by so many to be an actual translation of the Bible.

Again, *The Message* is not a translation of Scripture; it is just a book that has gained popularity by being endorsed by ministers of seeker-sensitive churches, who are aligned with the same type of agenda as outlined in the *Purpose-Driven Life*.

In my husband's book, **Brother Swaggart, How Can I Understand The Bible?**, he explains the meaning of true translation:

> Our present society is being flooded with so-called translations that are really interpretations or thought-for-thought translations, such as the Message Bible. Actually, these types of efforts cannot even be construed as Bibles. At best they are religious books.

> The only translation that can be concluded as the Word of God is a word-for-word translation, such as the King James. There are one or two other word-for-word translations; however, with these I am not familiar. But yet, there are several other things that need to be said about the King James translation.

> As we have already mentioned, the King James translation, despite being edited several times, still contains a fairly liberal usage of Elizabethan English. To all King James devotees, and I am one, it must be understood that the prophets and the apostles who were used by the Spirit of God to write the sacred text did not speak Elizabethan English. As well, when Matthew, Mark, Luke, and John

were originally written, the Words of Christ were not in red. These particular words in red are actually a marketing tool that was not used until the 20th century.

And again we emphasize that while the original manuscripts were most definitely inspired by the Holy Spirit and, thereby, error-free, doesn't mean that the translation is error-free.

No translation was inspired by the Holy Spirit, and none to my knowledge were claimed to be.

While there have been other translations from then until now, the King James is concluded by many scholars to be closer to the original text than any other effort. Down through the last several centuries, it, by far, has been the most widely used and widely known.

In this same book, my husband also offers a comprehensive chronology that tells the dramatic story of how the Bible was actually translated. The timeline stretches from 1500 B.C. when the Old Testament was put into writing to 1611 when the King James Version was completed — the version that has stood the test of time for more than 400 years.

Compare these centuries of translation work to Peterson's so-called translation efforts where he brags, "I did the Beatitudes in about 10 minutes."

When asked if Peterson actually uses *The Message* for his own personal devotions, he told *Christianity Today* no, he does not. What does that tell you?

BIBLE STUDY

Church, the best way to avoid the danger of a book like *The Message* is to read and study the Bible.

The Word of God tells us, *"Study to shew thyself approved unto God, a workman that needeth not to be ashamed, rightly dividing the word of truth"* (II Tim. 2:15).

Sometime back, my husband put together a list of ways for believers to best interpret the Bible. He said that anyone who will study these rules and use them as a basis for Bible study will find the Word of God opening up to him in a greater way.

The Lord will help you learn the Scriptures. As you consider the following study helps, let me close my portion of this chapter with a verse from the book of Luke:

"And they said one to another, Did not our heart burn within us, while He talked with us by the way, and while He opened to us the Scriptures?" (Lk. 24:32).

TWELVE RULES FOR INTERPRETATION OF THE BIBLE

1. Improve your ability in the tongue in which you read the Bible. For example, master the English language if the English Bible is to be used.
2. Accept the literal meanings of words. Apply to the Bible the same rules (grammar, figures of speech, types, symbols, allegories, parables, poetry, prophecy,

history) that you would to any form of human expression found outside the Bible.

3. Learn the manners, customs, and peculiar idioms of the periods during which the Bible was written.

4. Get acquainted with the geography of all Bible lands.

5. Acquire a general knowledge of the history of the Bible peoples and kingdoms so that you can understand Bible history as a whole.

6. Recognize the overall plan of the Bible: the ages and dispensations; the ultimate purpose of God to defeat Satan and restore man's dominion, rid the world of rebellion, and establish an eternal kingdom on earth ruled by God, Christ, and the resurrected saints.

7. Recognize the three classes of people dealt with in Scripture — the Jews, the Gentiles, and the church of our Lord Jesus Christ.

AND
SARAH
SAW

GRACE REVOLUTION
OR SIN REVOLUTION?

GRACE REVOLUTION OR SIN REVOLUTION?

I WOULD LIKE TO open this chapter with the following excerpt from The Expositor's Study Bible, taken from Hebrews 6:4-6:

> *For it is impossible for those who were once enlightened* (refers to those who have accepted the Light of the gospel, which means accepting Christ and His great sacrifice), *and have tasted of the heavenly gift* (pertains to Christ and what He did at the Cross), *and were made partakers of the Holy Spirit* (which takes place when a person comes to Christ),
>
> *And have tasted the good Word of God* (is not language that is used of an impenitent sinner, as some claim; the unsaved have no relish whatsoever for the truth of God, and see no beauty in it), *and the powers of the world to come* (refers to the work of the Holy Spirit within hearts and lives, which the unsaved cannot have or know),
>
> *If they shall fall away* (should have been translated, 'and having fallen away'), *to renew them again unto repentance*

('again' states they had once repented, but have now turned their backs on Christ); *seeing they crucify to themselves the Son of God afresh* (means they no longer believe what Christ did at the Cross, actually concluding Him to be an impostor; the only way any person can truly repent is to place his faith in Christ and the Cross; if that is denied, there is no repentance), *and put Him to an open shame* (means to hold Christ up to public ridicule; Paul wrote this epistle because some Christian Jews were going back into Judaism, or seriously contemplating doing so).

Every Christian can testify about how they came to receive the Lord Jesus Christ as their personal Saviour. They remember feeling the powerful conviction of the Holy Spirit. They remember repenting and asking the Lord to forgive them and how, afterward, feeling the relief and joy of restored fellowship with Him.

Most Christians realize that this is the same way the Lord deals with Christians when they sin: the Holy Spirit convicts us of sin and, out of a repentant heart, we confess that sin to the Lord, receive His forgiveness, and resume our fellowship and walk with the Lord.

A FALSE TEACHING

Unfortunately, there is a teaching that is becoming quite dominant in this country and elsewhere. It's referred to as the Grace Revolution, but in reality, it is an evolution away from the true grace of God.

In essence, this hyper-grace doctrine claims that the Cross of Christ addressed all sin, past, present, and future, which is exactly correct. Most definitely, the Cross did do this. But then it states that when a Christian sins, due to the fact that all future sins have been atoned as well, the believer does not have to confess his sin, or ask forgiveness, or even mention it at all.

In other words, just go on as if though nothing has ever happened. Plain and simple this is error. And as all error does, sooner or later it will cause the believer terrible problems. In fact, some will even lose their souls.

The foundation of this false doctrine claims that I John 1:9 is speaking to sinners only and not saints, and that Christians do not — and should not — confess their sins to the Lord.

KNOWN SIN UNCONFESSED IS SIN UNFORGIVEN

In The Expositor's Study Bible, I John 1:9 says:

If we confess our sins *(pertains to acts of sin, whatever they might be; the sinner is to believe [Jn. 3:16]; the saint is to confess)*, He *(the Lord)* is faithful and just to forgive us our sins *(God will always be true to His own nature and promises, keeping faith with Himself and with man)*, and to cleanse us from all unrighteousness. *('All,' not some. All sin was remitted, paid for, and put away on the basis of the satisfaction offered for the demands of God's holy law, which sinners broke, when the Lord Jesus died on the Cross.)*

As my husband put so well in these expository notes, "the

sinner is to believe; the saint is to confess." So my question is this: are there really born-again believers who think that they no longer have to confess their sins to the Lord?

OPPOSED TO THE FALSE DOCTRINE, NOT THE PEOPLE TEACHING IT

Rather than name the false teachers of this hyper-grace doctrine and list their gross error regarding unconfessed sin, I want to quote instead from the commentary my husband wrote concerning I John 1:9 as I think it will be a great benefit to you.

He writes:

The phrase, 'If we confess our sins,' pertains to acts of sin, whatever they might be. No Christian has to sin; however, the sad truth is, every single Christian does, at times, sin.

'Confess' in the Greek is *homologeo*, and means 'to say the same thing as another,' or, 'to agree with another.' Confession of sin on the part of the saint means, therefore, to say the same thing that God does about that sin, to agree with God as to all the implication of that sin as it relates to the Christian who commits it and to a Holy God against whom it is committed (Wuest).

All of this includes the saint's hatred of that sin, his sense of guilt because of it, his contrition because of it, the determination to put it out of his life, which can be done only by understanding that all victory is in the Cross, and that our faith must ever be in that finished work. In fact, the very reason that we sin is because we get our eyes off of the Cross (Lk. 9:23-24) and onto other things.

The English word *confess* means 'to admit the truth of an accusation, to own up to the fact that one is guilty of having committed the sin.' But the Greek word means far more than that, as we have addressed above.

The Greek word teaches that the constant attitude of the saint towards sin should be one of a contrite heart, ever eager to have the Holy Spirit to point out all wrong, and to put it out of the life by the power of that same Holy Spirit.

To whom are we to confess our sins? We are to confess them to the One who is going to forgive us, namely the Lord. Also, if we have harmed someone else, we should confess our wrong to that person as well.

In fact, the very moment that we do something wrong, the Holy Spirit without fail, will convict us (Jn. 16:8). At that moment we should confess our sin to the Lord, whatever it might be, and wherever we might be. This is a matter of the heart, so it does not need ceremony of any kind.

But what if the Christian does not confess his sin? Failing to confess his sin to God means that the Lord at the same time, cannot forgive such a sin, which leaves the believer in a precarious situation. Forgiveness by God, in the context of which the Holy Spirit here speaks, is not automatic. It requires confession of our sin to Him and for many and varied reasons.

The believer is to never take sin lightly. In fact, there is really nothing anyone can do to make amends for sin. All we can do is to acknowledge our guilt and turn to God for forgiveness.

As well, there is really nothing we can do to make up for the hurt we cause others, other than mutually extending and accepting forgiveness. However, if we have harmed someone else in any way, and refuse to confess our wrong-doing to that person, John plainly says that such a person 'walks in darkness' (I Jn. 2:11). Jesus said, 'Therefore your sin remaineth' (Jn. 9:41).

Any Christian who sins, and refuses to confess that sin to the Lord, or sins against a brother or sister and re-fuses to confess the wrongdoing to the individual, asking forgiveness, is in serious spiritual trouble indeed! If that person continues on in such a state, it is impossible but that spiritual deterioration must be the case. As it regards the salvation of such a person, I'll have to leave that to the Lord; however, it should be well understood that we are speaking here of very serious things."

I think this commentary makes it perfectly clear that I John 1:9 is speaking about believers and not sinners, as this hyper-grace teaching claims.

Another claim of this false doctrine — and perhaps even most dangerous to the believer — is this: that the Holy Spirit does not convict believers when they sin.

As my husband pointed out on his program, *The Message*

of the Cross, if sin is present in a Christian's heart, the Holy Spirit will absolutely convict that believer:

"Whenever you do something wrong, and it's obvious that it's wrong, you feel it in your spirit. You sense it. The Holy Spirit is grieved. The Holy Spirit convicts you of that thing you did wrong.

A child of God is not saved in sin, he's saved from sin. And while sin may be something that happens once in a while, it is not a constant occurrence in the heart and life of the believer. If there is something wrong, the Holy Spirit convicts you, where you are.

When Simon Peter denied the Lord, and Jesus came by and looked at him; Peter went out and wept bitterly — that was the Holy Spirit convicting Peter of what he had done."

My husband and I feel so strongly about the dangers surrounding this false doctrine, that we've been using every opportunity to warn Christians who may have gotten tangled up in this wrong teaching. That's why we've been discussing it on our SBN programs, *The Message of the Cross* and *Frances & Friends*. My husband also addressed this error of unconfessed sin in his book, *Elijah*, and the following excerpt fits so well here:

> Repentance is admitting the wrong, condemning oneself and totally justifying God. It is completely turning around from the erroneous direction that one has been traveling.
>
> Repentance is seldom engaged by the church, simply because it is an ugly business. One has to admit wrongdoing. It seems that only the most destitute can do so.

Actually, at this particular time repentance is such a rarity in the modern church that the church really does not even know what to do with one who repents. Due to a plethora of man-made rules, repentance toward God is not even recognized, only repentance toward man. God will not accept repentance toward man simply because it is God who has been offended by our sin. There is not a single Christian denomination in America and Canada, at least of which I am aware, that will accept repentance toward God.

Every single one, again, of which I am aware, completely ignores the Word of God, makes up its own rules, which by and large deny repentance. Repentance is always toward God and never toward man. While it certainly may be true that repentance toward God may include the asking of forgiveness of man, still, all sin is in its conception directed toward God.

TRUTH AND ERROR

One of Satan's chiefest ploys is to mix some truth in with error. The truth serves as bait, with the believer then thinking that all that is said must be correct. So the fact that error contains some truth doesn't make it acceptable at all. So the believer has to listen very carefully to what he is hearing. And to be sure, the idea that a Christian doesn't need to confess his sin to the Lord whenever sin is committed, is facetious indeed!

ALL SIN IS AGAINST GOD

The believer must understand the truth of our heading, in that all sin is ultimately against God. Considering that when we sin we have offended Him, means that we have to ask forgiveness for that sin.

WHAT HAPPENS TO A CHRISTIAN WHO BELIEVES THIS LIE?

What you're asking concerns the believer who believes this error, never asks forgiveness for anything that he's done that's wrong, and what will be the results?

God is patient, loving and kind. He doesn't throw us over when we make a mistake, or when we do something foolish. He seeks to bring us back to the fold. However, when one fails the Lord in any capacity, even in the act of refusing to confess our sin to Him, relationship is somewhat hindered. It cannot be otherwise. God is the judge, however, if the believer continues on that erroneous path, there will come a time that the wrong direction will reap it's results, and it won't be pretty.

Ladies and gentlemen, this false doctrine is by no means a revolution of grace but, more accurately, a revolution sin. My husband and I believe that this is one of Satan's biggest efforts to hinder the Message of the Cross — the true message of grace. The response we are receiving on this subject from our SBN audience indicate that many Christians are migrating toward this false doctrine.

As a Christian, if you find yourself struggling with this deception, I would encourage you to go to the Lord in prayer and sincerely ask Him to help you discern what is right and what is wrong. Ask Him for His leading, His help, and His guidance because the most important thing in the world is to be right with Him. I believe the Lord will answer that prayer and lead you to correct doctrine, the correct teaching, and the correct way.

I'll close this chapter with the following verses from the book of James:

> *Brethren, if any of you do err from the truth* (James is speaking here of believers, and of them straying from the truth of the Cross), *and one convert him* (refers to strengthening the individual, turning him back to the right way of truth, which is back to Christ and the Cross);
>
> *Let him know, that he which converts the sinner from the error of his way* (bluntly proclaims any way other than the Cross as the 'way of sin,' which then makes the one traveling such a way 'a sinner') *shall save a soul from death, and shall hide a multitude of sins.* (This refers to the fact that if the believer leaves the Cross, thereby transferring his faith to something else, and such an erring way is continued, it will result in the loss of the soul. To pull one back to the Cross saves that soul, which the Cross alone can do!) (James 5:19-20).

AND SARAH SAW

SPIRITUAL UNITY vs.
SOCIAL UNITY

CHAPTER NINETEEN

SPIRITUAL UNITY vs. SOCIAL UNITY

THE BIBLE ADMONISHES BELIEVERS to strive for the unity of the faith, and to do so continually and diligently:

Psalms 133:1: *"Behold, how good and how pleasant it is for brethren to dwell together in unity!"*

Ephesians 4:3: *"Endeavoring to keep the unity of the Spirit in the bond of peace."*

Ephesians 4:13: *"Till we all come in the unity of the faith, and of the knowledge of the Son of God, unto a perfect man, unto the measure of the stature of the fullness of Christ."*

Jude, Vs. 3: *"Beloved, when I gave all diligence to write unto you of the common salvation, it was needful for me to write unto you, and exhort you that you should earnestly contend for the faith which was once delivered unto the saints."*

The meaning of the word *unity* as it is brought forth throughout Scripture clearly speaks of spiritual unity — a unity of belief. If believers are to work together successfully to further the cause of Christ, they must be of like-spirit and of like-faith. Believers must first be in agreement regarding essential biblical doctrine because it is the doctrine a person believes that will influence his spirit. Different spirits are uncomfortable together, but like-spirits bond effortlessly.

Let's look at it this way: The doctrine one believes essentially determines which god he worships. Thus, his spirit will be influenced by the very nature of that deity. The Christian comes to know the true Lord through the doctrines of Scripture. Jesus Christ Himself was the Word made flesh. If the church does not have unity in biblical doctrine, it cannot have unity in the Spirit. And, let it be known, there is only one Holy Spirit.

"God is a Spirit: and they who worship Him must worship Him in spirit and in truth" (Jn. 4:24).

Unfortunately today, many are trying to change the spiritual unity of the church to a social unity, which will not be able to maintain the divine fortitude needed to withstand the coming evil days. Lord, help us to be unified in your Holy Spirit rather than in our humanity.

NEOORTHODOX LANGUAGE

Insisting upon the true spiritual unity of the faith is among the greatest of every believer's responsibilities until Christ's return. God's Word tells us that this truth will constantly come under attack. False teachings will attempt to change the simple gospel message and destroy the salvation of many.

"Now the Spirit speaks expressly, that in the latter times some shall depart from the faith, giving heed to seducing

spirits, and doctrines of devils" (I Tim. 4:1).

But in the church today, the unity we are striving for has been subtly redefined, and this false community-based social unity actually ends up working directly against the true unity of the faith. The strategy of using neoorthodox language to deceive the public is actually quite common among those who wish to further liberalize the church and the world. It takes terminology, whose definitions were accepted in the past because of their accuracy, and begins misapplying these traditional terms to new ideas.

People end up accepting the new idea based on familiar language before they realize it is being used completely out of context. The idea that there can be unity in the church despite differences of belief regarding the essential doctrines of salvation is perhaps the biggest farce being perpetuated in the modern church. The Lord plainly rebukes such an attitude.

"Can two walk together, except they be agreed?" (Amos 3:3).

However, what we are hearing espoused from pulpits across America today is a siren call to lay down our differences and labor toward common goals.

THE MESSAGE OF THE CROSS IS THE CURE

This enchanting love song promises us refuge from the crashing waves of the persecution we endure for the cause of Christ, persecution which comes from both the world and our apostate brethren. It promises that we no longer have to separate ourselves from those who are teaching false doctrine and from those who insist that their lifestyle of sin is accepted by God. Come, they say, and let us work together to end the world's hunger, fight incurable diseases, and provide counseling for victims of natural disasters. Let's show the world how much Christians really care.

But this will not really cause anyone to recognize the true value of the Christian faith. Many other social institutions, religious organizations, and celebrity charities provide aid for those in need. Besides, it is at this point that the labor of the church has ceased from being categorized as Christian.

Remember, the real work of Christianity is the preservation and evangelization of the correct biblical doctrine — the message of Christ and Him crucified! Our work is to lift up the name of Jesus and tear down the useless ideas of men.

"Casting down imaginations, and every high thing that exalts itself against the knowledge of God, and bringing into captivity every thought to the obedience of Christ" (II Cor. 10:5).

Humanity cannot be adequately helped if the cause of its problems has not been addressed, and this is where the church was meant to shine as a genuine light of hope for the world. The true church is the only establishment on earth capable of identifying the real problem and proclaiming the real solution! Christians are to joyfully proclaim this pure and undefiled message: Sin is the cause for humanity's ills, but the Message of the Cross is the cure!

But we have turned our backs on this work and instead adopted a false unity that can accomplish nothing more than humanistic social service. Truly our labor is in vain.

"For this cause, when I could no longer forbear, I sent to know your faith, lest by some means the tempter have tempted you, and our labour be in vain" (I Thess. 3:5).

SOCIAL UNITY?

Rick Warren made this statement in issue #337 of his Ministry Tool Box: "As pastors, as shepherds of God's people, it's our job to protect our congregations from Satan's greatest weapon — disunity. It's not always easy, but it's what we've been called to do."

At first glance, most Christians would agree. As we have already explained, disunity of faith is indeed a work of evil; it is the same as being disunified with Christ. However, Rick Warren has tricked his followers because he is not speaking of spiritual unity here, but rather social unity.

Disunity of faith is not the kind that threatens Rick Warren. His real concern is that the believers who are striving for spiritual unity will discover that many of his programs and plans do not line up with the Word. So, he must silence the mouths of these who would attempt to point out these errors. These people must be labeled as "bad guys" or "troublemakers."

Watch how Warren twists Scripture to work against these who are taking seriously their call to maintain the purity of the faith. He quotes Titus 3:10 from the New International Version of the Bible which states, *"Warn a divisive person once, and then warn him a second time. After that, have nothing to do with him."*

Warren says this means that after two warnings, a pastor may have to remove a divisive person from his church. But, what is meant by "divisive?" Of course, Rick Warren is referring to those who refuse to comply with his established church programs, even if they are unscriptural.

However, if we look at the King James Version of the Bible, we can clearly see what the Lord really meant by a divisive person. The KJV says, *"A man that is an heretic after the first and second admonition reject."* A heretic speaks of one who is out of unity spiritually-speaking, not socially-speaking. This is another reason many of the modern translations of the Bible can be very dangerous. False prophets can use their wording to further deceive the people and continue in their ungodly directions.

THE BLIND LEAD THE BLIND!

The Bible's definition of unity and Rick Warren's definition of unity are not the same. Warren's definition means the elimination of all questioning regarding the methods or leadership of the church, even if such would ultimately work to preserve true faith.

Therefore, he has also eliminated from his congregation any sense of individualism or the ability to think for oneself. He has placed a false social unity above the truth of God's Word, and made people like the Bereans the ultimate sinners in the eyes of the people. The believers in Berea were commended in the Bible for their insistence that any teaching brought to them be biblically accurate (Acts 17:11).

Warren's *Purpose-Driven* church, which does not allow room for believers to strive for the unity of faith, instead functions on manipulative consensus-thinking. This is not unity; it is brainwashing!

It uses peer pressure as a guiding force to keep inquisitive individuals in line. But, Jesus said, *"And if the blind lead the blind, both shall fall into the ditch"* (Mat. 15:14).

THE WRONG KIND OF UNITY

Pope Benedict also believes in the wrong kind of unity which he made clear in his Angelus Address in St. Peter's Square on Jan. 20, 2008. Speaking to a crowd of approximately 200,000 people, the pope spoke concerning that special "Week of Prayer for Christian Unity."

He encouraged believers to "never grow tired of praying for unity among Christians!" But look, this next statement shows that the unity he speaks of is social, not spiritual, because it excludes doctrinal agreement. An online article in the Catholic News Agency states: "During this week of prayer, Catholics, Orthodox, Anglicans, and Protestants, 'implore the Lord together, in a more intense way, for the gift of communion,' the Pontiff reminded the faithful ... 'The evangelical mission of the Church is thus an ecumenical walk, a journey of unity in faith, in evangelical witness and authentic fraternity.'"

The term *ecumenical* speaks of a worldwide scope or applicability. Members of differing faiths strive to find possible commonalities among them and agree to respect one another's spiritual journeys. But, true Christians cannot do this when they know another's belief will send him to hell; Christians are compelled to speak the truth in love.

On October 27, 1986, in Assisi, Italy, Pope John Paul II began one of the greatest ecumenical movements in history. He gathered the leaders of the world's most prominent religions to pray for peace, espousing that they were all praying to the same god despite their differences of belief. Remember, though, that this is impossible because it is doctrine that will determine which god you worship.

John Paul II later allowed the Dali Lama to place a Buddha on the altar for a Buddhist worship ceremony to take place there at a Catholic Church.

RE-THOUGHT AND REINVENTED?

Even more religious leaders are promoting this false social unity, which is void of spiritual truth. On January 17-19, 2008, a large conference took place at Robert Schuller's Crystal Cathedral and was attended by many well-known pastors and other secular leaders, such as Erwin McManus, Chuck Colson, Rupert Murdoch, Kay Warren, Gary Smalley, Henry Cloud, George Barna, Bishop Charles E. Blake, Jim Burns, former president George H. W. Bush, Dr. Tim Clinton, Phil Cooke, George Foreman, Jon Gordon, Dr. Michael

Guillen, Lou Holtz, Dan Kimball, Larry King, H. B. London, Jr., Jay Sekulow, Ben Stein, Lee Strobel, and many others.

The conference was entitled "Rethink," where the obvious goal of the meeting would be to find unity among religions, even if it means finding it outside of biblical teaching and truth.

One observer of the conference wrote: "For nearly two thousand years, most professing Christians have seen the Bible as the foundation for the Christian faith. The overall view at the Rethink Conference, however, is that Christianity, as we have known it, has run its course and must be replaced ... Speakers insisted that Christianity must be re-thought and reinvented if the name of Jesus Christ is going to survive here on planet Earth now that we are in the 21st century."

UNITY OUTSIDE OF TRUTH?

This is a horrifying example of forsaking spiritual unity for social unity! What could be more dangerous or have any greater eternal consequence than to re-think the truth? God's Word is the eternal, absolute truth, which has never changed and never will change. Any conference worth having would further clarify, celebrate, and reaffirm the truth, not reinvent it!

Unity outside of the truth will ultimately unify people in the one place none of them wish to go. No words can describe the hatred they will feel toward one another when they realize it was this fellowship that put them in the eternal torment of hell. The sacrifice of spiritual unity was not worth their temporary social benefits on earth. They fought the wrong battle!

If they had only heeded these clear admonitions of Scripture rather than accepting various spiritual paths, they might have saved their souls:

"Fight the good fight of faith, lay hold on eternal life, whereunto you are also called, and have professed a good profession before many witnesses" (I Tim. 6:12).

"And that from a child you have known the holy Scriptures, which are able to make you wise unto salvation through faith which is in Christ Jesus" (II Tim. 3:15).

AND SARAH SAW

CHAPTER 20

CHURCH OF SILENCE

CHURCH OF SILENCE

A CONSPIRACY OF SILENCE is controlling the modern church. Many believers who used to love God are being destroyed because of false teachings that are rampant in the church, but no one is allowed to talk about it.

Modern believers are preconditioned, or should I say brainwashed, thinking that if they point out someone teaching false doctrine, they are a troublemaker, or worse, a religious bigot.

They are shamed into silence, and in so doing, choose their own deaths as they leave false teachers free as birds to spread their poisonous doctrines. Remember, *"A little leaven leaveneth the whole lump"* (Gal. 5:9).

Prayerfully, there will soon be a remnant of the Lord who will be able to assuage this false guilt and condemnation put upon them by the enemy and his followers. Hopefully, this remnant will have the fire of God shut up in their bones, which will overcome and speak the truth no matter the opposition (Jer. 20:9).

In fact, the truth is that if any one of us preaches anything contrary to what the Bible teaches, cries should go up from other pulpits all over the country, but shepherds are no longer protecting the sheep. Instead, pastors today stare off into space like zombies, refusing to spot the wolves, whether the wolves infiltrate as leaders or laymen.

We must ask ourselves, however, if such men are true shepherds because Jesus told us: *"But he that is an hireling, and not the shepherd ... Sees the wolf coming, and leaves the sheep ... The hireling flees, because he is an hireling, and cares not for the sheep"* (Jn. 10:12-13).

Perhaps, if you are one such shepherd who prefers leaving your sheep to the wolves, you should try fleeing your pulpit first.

THE SILENCE IS DEAFENING

Christians today are also being told that they need to fellowship with and work with men who do not know God, men whose doctrines are just as unscriptural as those of the Pharisees. In the process, of course, discerning believers are not supposed to rebuke such men for any of their doctrinal compromises. Yes, the silence is deafening. People are failing to hear the truth. Don't you know, believer, that Christ gave you authority in His name to silence demons? They aren't supposed to silence you: *"And when the devil was cast out, the dumb spoke"* (Mat. 9:33).

And in accordance with this devilish conspiracy, our Lord and Saviour is also being presented today as if he had been a Pharisee's doormat — as if He was only meek, lowly, kind, and very loving to the false teachers.

This, however, is a totally false picture of the Jesus Christ of the Bible.

Have we forgotten about the day Jesus drove the moneychangers out of the temple with a whip (Jn. 2:15)? When Jesus dealt with false teachers, His words were sharp, even harsh at times, and His actions were completely plain. No one could have misunderstood.

LOYALTY TO THE WORD

Jesus did not sugarcoat anything, turn a blind eye, or leave anyone with a false impression. In Matthew 23:23-34, false preachers were called hypocrites, blind guides, blind, whited sepulchers, serpents, and a generation of vipers.

Dear Christian, just because someone is a high-ranking leader in the church doesn't put him above mistakes, much less make him a god. When the people tried to worship the disciples due to the miracles God worked through them, Barnabas and Paul were tremendously grieved and asked the people, *"Sirs, why do you these things? We also are men of like passions with you"* (Acts 14:15).

At times a religious leader happens to be a true man of God who is temporarily deceived, and sometimes he is an actual wolf in sheep's clothing. Either way, your loyalty must always be to God and His truth, not to human leadership.

Christ, in fact, admonished true believers to do what is right in the sight of the Lord even when our leadership does not.

"Then spoke Jesus to the multitude, and to His disciples, saying, The scribes and the Pharisees sit in Moses' seat: all therefore whatsoever they bid you observe, that observe and do; but do not ye after their works: for they say, and do not" (Mat. 23:1-3).

A FORM OF GODLINESS

The church at Ephesus was commended because they had *"tried them which say they are apostles, and are not, and hast found them liars"* (Rev. 2:2).

The church at Pergamos was rebuked because they tolerated those that held *"the doctrine of Balaam"* and the *"doctrine of the Nicolaitans, which thing I hate"* (Rev. 2:14-15). God hates the doctrines of men, so it is never right to tolerate a false teacher.

Men who teach unscriptural doctrines are to be tried, judged, or both by the Word of God and exposed expressly as false teachers. Unfortunately, preachers today seek every means possible to avoid their duty to discern and judge, despite the light given to us in Scripture regarding such.

Romans 16:17: *"Now I beseech you, brethren, mark them who cause divisions and offences contrary to the doctrine which you have* learned (refers to the fact that false teachers are to be identified); *and avoid them* (turn away from and shun these)."

We are also to rebuke them: *"This witness is true. Wherefore rebuke them sharply, that they may be sound in the faith"* (Titus 1:13).

We are to have no fellowship with them: *"And have no fellowship with the unfruitful works of darkness, but rather reprove them"* (Eph. 5:11).

We are to withdraw from them: *"Now we command you, brethren, in the name of our Lord Jesus Christ, that you withdraw yourselves from every brother who walks disorderly, and not after the tradition which he received of us. For yourselves know how you ought to follow us: for we behaved not ourselves disorderly among you"* (II Thess. 3:6-7).

We are not to receive them into our house: *"If there come any unto you, and bring not this doctrine, receive him not into your house, neither bid him God speed: for he who bids him God speed is partaker of his evil deeds"* (II Jn. 1:10-11).

We are to turn away from them: *"Having a form of godliness, but denying the power thereof: from such turn away. For of this sort are they which creep into houses, and lead captive silly women laden with sins, led away with divers lusts, ever learning, and never able to come to the knowledge of the truth"* (II Tim. 3:5-7).

Now, how can believers turn away from false teachers if we do not identify them?

COMPARE IT WITH THE WORD

Every message we hear must be compared to the Word of God. A true man of God will always do this.

"Preach the Word; be instant in season, out of season;

reprove, rebuke, exhort with all longsuffering and doctrine" (II Tim. 4:2).

God-called men and women are to be just as faithful as Paul was in the task of exposing false ministers and openly rejecting their messages. We are to judge their Jesus, their spirit, and their gospel by the Word of God: *"By the Word of Truth, by the power of God, by the armour of righteousness on the right hand and on the left"* (II Cor. 6:7).

Look at II Corinthians 11:13: *"For such are false apostles, deceitful workers, transforming themselves into the apostles of Christ."*

Then verses 14-15: *"And no marvel; for Satan himself is transformed into an angel of light. Therefore it is no great thing if his ministers also be transformed as the ministers of righteousness; whose end shall be according to their works."*

Paul says these preachers are ministers of Satan. False doctrine is, therefore, not to be brought into our homes in any fashion. We must guard what we allow into the hearts and minds of both ourselves and our loved ones. In other words, we should not read the literature of false teachers, listen to their music, or listen to them by radio or television. The enemy is too sly; we should not give him room: *"Neither give place to the Devil"* (Eph. 4:27).

FALSE TEACHERS

God's Word goes even further and tells us we are to

separate ourselves from false teachers. God's people must come out of apostasy and religious error. Paul did not hesitate to stand strong and firm. Consider these examples:

Paul once had to name Peter publicly:

"But when Peter was come to Antioch, I withstood him to the face, because he was to be blamed. For before that certain came from James, he did eat with the Gentiles: but when they were come, he withdrew and separated himself, fearing them which were of the circumcision. And the other Jews dissembled likewise with him; insomuch that Barnabas also was carried away with their dissimulation. But when I saw that they walked not uprightly according to the truth of the gospel, I said unto Peter before them all, If you, being a Jew, live after the manner of Gentiles, and not as do the Jews, why do you compel the Gentiles to live as do the Jews?" (Gal. 2:11-14).

Paul named Demas:

"For Demas has forsaken me, having loved this present world, and is departed unto Thessalonica" (II Tim. 4:10).

Paul named Hymenaeus and Alexander:

"This charge I commit unto you, son Timothy, according to the prophecies which went before on you, that you by them might war a good warfare; holding faith, and a good conscience; which some having put away concerning faith have made shipwreck: of whom is Hymenaeus and Alexander; whom I have delivered unto Satan, that they may learn not to blaspheme" (I Tim. 1:18-20).

Paul named Hymenaeus and Philetus:

"Study to show yourself approved unto God, a workman who needs not to be ashamed, rightly dividing the Word of Truth. But shun profane and vain babblings: for they will increase unto more ungodliness. And their word will eat as does a canker: of whom is Hymenaeus and Philetus; who concerning the truth have erred, saying that the resurrection is past already; and overthrow the faith of some" (II Tim. 2:15-18).

You see, false doctrine causes Christians to stumble and lose their way with God. This is the reason we must expose it. Here are a few more examples:

Paul also named Alexander the coppersmith because he was the enemy of truth:

"Alexander the coppersmith did me much evil: the Lord reward him according to his works: of whom you beware also; for he has greatly withstood our words" (II Tim. 4:14-15).

John named Diotrephes:

"I wrote unto the church: but Diotrephes, who loves to have the preeminence among them, receives us not. Wherefore, if I come, I will remember his deeds which he does, prating against us with malicious words: and not content therewith, neither does he himself receive the brethren, and forbids them who would, and casts them out of the church. Beloved, follow not that which is evil, but that which is good. He who does good is of God: but he who does evil has not seen God" (III Jn. 1:9-11).

Moses called the name of Balaam:

"He sent messengers therefore unto Balaam the son of Beor to Pethor, which is by the river of the land of the children of his people, to call him, saying, Behold, there is a people come out from Egypt: behold, they cover the face of the earth, and they abide over against me" (Num. 22:5). Jude exposed the error of Balaam: *"Woe unto them! for they have gone in the way of Cain, and ran greedily after the error of Balaam for reward, and perished in the gainsaying of Core"* (Jude 1:11).

Nathan identified the man:

"And Nathan said to David, You are the man. Thus says the Lord *God of Israel, I anointed you king over Israel, and I delivered you out of the hand of Saul"* (II Sam. 12:7).

DANGEROUS

The world of religion has become quite dangerous as false teachers have broken down the barrier of separation between God's people and false religions.

In some ways king Jehoshaphat was a good king, but he did not practice separation, causing his son to marry the wicked king Ahab's daughter. Jehu named king Jehoshaphat for his error. Read II Chronicles 18:1-21. In verses 1 through 6 of this chapter, Jehoshaphat made an alliance with Ahab and went to battle with him, but he was rebuked by a man of God.

"And Jehu the son of Hanani the seer went out to meet him, and said to king Jehoshaphat, Should you help the

*ungodly, and love them who hate the LORD? therefore is
wrath upon you from before the LORD"* (II Chron. 19:2).

We could ask that question today: "Is the church to partner with ungodly religions even if the motive is to help cure
AIDS or other social problems?" No!

In the first place, we can't cure any problem, but secondly,
because partnering with the ungodly will only lead to apostasy, just as Jehoshaphat found out the hard way. Thank God,
we later find Jehoshaphat repenting and going out among the
people to bring them back to God.

*"And Jehoshaphat dwelt at Jerusalem: and he went
out again through the people from Beer-sheba to Mount
Ephraim, and brought them back unto the LORD God of
their fathers"* (II Chron. 19:4).

TWISTING OF SCRIPTURE

Rick Warren tells the church today that we are to partner
with false religions in the spirit of cooperation for the common good of all Americans. Those who love God know better
than this! The church was not established for this purpose.
Warren, however, grossly twists Scripture to try to justify
working with the unsaved crowd.

Referring to Matthew, Chapter 10, Warren says that,
"There's a man of peace in every village, in every government,
in every business, in every church ... When you find the man
of peace, if he's open and he's willing to work with you, you
bless him and you start your work there ... The man of peace is

open and influential ... The man of peace does not have to be a Christian believer. Could be a Muslim. Could be Jewish."

This is not what Matthew, Chapter 10, teaches. *"And if the house be worthy, let your peace come upon it: but if it be not worthy, let your peace return to you"* (Mat. 10:13).

You see, false teachers have to misuse Scripture to promote their private agendas and interests. They want as many people as possible to follow them, but they don't care about their spiritual condition. The Lord, on the other hand, is concerned with the souls of lost people rather than the manpower those people can offer.

"Say not you, There are yet four months, and then cometh harvest? behold, I say unto you, Lift up your eyes, and look on the fields; for they are white already to harvest" (Jn. 4:35).

Ladies and gentlemen, the massive social works of apostate religious leaders have nothing to do with the true work of God.

AND SARAH SAW

CHAPTER 21

IF IT WERE POSSIBLE,
THEY SHALL DECEIVE

IF IT WERE POSSIBLE,
THEY SHALL DECEIVE

FOR THERE SHALL ARISE false Christs, and false prophets, and shall show great signs and wonders; insomuch that, if it were possible, they shall deceive the very elect (Mat. 24:24).

On Saturday morning, Jan. 8, 2011, people in Tucson City, Arizona, gathered in the parking lot of a Safeway supermarket to hear U.S. Congresswoman Gabrielle Giffords who was holding a "Congress on Your Corner" meeting. Shortly after 10 a.m., a gunman opened fire and killed six people and wounded 13 others, including Giffords, who was shot in the head.

Four days later, a memorial service was held for the victims on the University of Arizona campus. As I watched this service, an Indian spiritual leader performed his ritual, raising feathers to bless the doors of the building. Of course, this concerned me greatly, but I assured myself that they would have a minister of the gospel pray and say some comforting words to the families of the victims who were present. But that didn't happen.

GOD HELP US!

I received the following email that quotes a pastor who was present at the memorial service in Tucson. This is what he had to say:

> I sat with my mouth open last night at the so-called 'memorial' service in Tucson, and couldn't believe my eyes or my ears at what I was hearing and seeing — even before President Obama spoke.
>
> Think about it: They had a band that played 'Fanfare To The Common Man,' a chorus group, an Indian spiritual leader who raised feathers to bless the doors of the building, two government officials who read from the Bible, including lesbian Janet Napolitano, and the Scriptures they used had nothing to do with the evil of man or the goodness of God or His ability to provide comfort to those who were in grief.
>
> Then the President's remarks were about the goodness and the ideals of man. He quoted Job: 'When I looked for light, then came darkness' — supposedly trying to connect his search for answers to what happened, but found none! The president's remarks were interrupted more than 50 times with applause, whistles, yells, and such, and the 24,000 attendees could pick up their t-shirt on the way out!
>
> I tried to put all of that into perspective, but then it dawned on me: This is the 'global church' in full color! Not one

preacher, not one hymn, not one request for God's presence, power, or permission to come into His presence! God help us!

GLOBALISM

As I read that email, my concern turned into shock. This person is right. This truly was a model, a blueprint for a global church service! This is a picture of what we will be forced to tolerate if the American people are not able to stop the march toward globalism. This event was a fast-forward move toward a one-world government and a one-world church.

Jesus Christ and true Christianity are falling speedily by the wayside. There has been absolutely no outcry from any ministry or government official regarding this, and the media did not offer one word of criticism. And shockingly, the president's approval ratings went up! Obama is indeed a good communicator, but so was Hitler, and so will be the Antichrist. The Antichrist will be able to seduce the multitude with smooth words.

BLINDNESS

Church, we've got to pray because of the blindness that has fallen on the American people; their blinders have to be removed, and their eyes have got to be opened before it's too late.

The Scripture that Obama did read from Job was taken

out of context, and even sarcastically implied that when the God of the Bible is sought, He cannot be found and that the God of the Bible does not answer the cries of His children.

This should have been offensive to believers, but instead, most of the church was pacified simply because the Bible was read. Again, wake up church! When someone opens God's Holy Word, it's not meant to be a bedtime story. You should be actively listening, discerning whether the reader has presented what the Holy Spirit intended.

Also, the t-shirts that were draped across the backs of the chairs at the service read, "Together we thrive." Sound familiar? To me this is just another manipulative push toward the censorship of any person who disagrees with the policies and behavior of this current administration. I would also add that this is a censorship upon any person or group who disagrees with the leadership or direction of the modern day church. Contemporary church leaders coach us to stay in unity while accepting anything and everything. We are expected to believe that "together we thrive" despite the unbiblical and ungodly teachings in our midst.

Now, I want to contrast this with something that happened during one of our share-a-thons.

JESUS IS EVERYTHING

On the second day of a particular share-a-thon, a song was played from one of our campmeetings, "To Me He Has Become Everything," speaking about the Lord Jesus Christ.

As the presence of God began to move through the airwaves, people began to worship the Lord Jesus Christ. We continued to play this single song for the rest of the entire day and late into the night.

A MOVE OF GOD

People had to pull their cars to the side of the road. Others in their homes could do nothing but walk through their house worshipping and praising God. Others at work had to continue their task with tears streaming down their cheeks and praise and worship flowing through their hearts. Other people were healed, saved, some were filled with the Holy Spirit, and many said that they had never before had such an encounter with God.

Our employees at the ministry were also touched and moved upon by the Holy Spirit. One worker wrote about it and shared the following with the entire staff at Jimmy Swaggart Ministries:

As I sit at my computer watching this campmeeting service, I can't help but think about how the Lord has used this service and song to bless the viewers and the ministry itself.

See, what many of us who work at the ministry do not realize is that one decision, and the right people, can be the catalyst for the Lord to move in a miraculous way. When a few people received the request late yesterday afternoon to make this song available for this morning's share-a-thon shift, who could have ever imagined the magnitude of that decision? The Lord used a combination of a few people who happened to be working late in the TV department to get this service out and ready for the next morning. And oh, what a morning it turned out to be.

I said all that to say this: I have worked at Jimmy Swaggart Ministries for over 15 years now and in this time the Lord has had to 'grow me up' and teach me His way and how to trust Him for everything. I could never have imagined what the Lord was preparing the entire ministry for.

We watched and learned as the Lord prepared the message that was to be proclaimed. We watched as the method for that message to go out was raised up — the SonLife Radio Network. We watched in amazement as the birth of modern technology allowed us to reach the entire world through the means of the Internet. And, in the last year, we watched as the Lord moved to establish the SonLife Broadcasting Network.

At an exponential rate, the Lord opened doors for this new Christian television network to reach an unprecedented number of people in such a short amount of time. During the first share-a-thon where the people were asked to help support the ministry with a goal of $1 million, the Lord met the need and put His seal of approval on this all-important task.

I will never forget what Brother Swaggart said immediately after the goal was met. He said, 'The Lord has just assured us that this is His will. Now we have to make sure and walk softly before Him in everything we do.'

I think this is something that we all need to remember: Jimmy Swaggart Ministries is ordained by God. Our mission statement is from the throne room of heaven. Our goal is to win the lost. We have one mandate: souls. The world is hurting and lost. But now, more than ever, the church is hurting. The recurring statement from our viewers and supporters is that they have been in a 'wilderness,' and the presence of the Lord is changing their lives through SonLife Broadcasting.

Everything we do should be done as unto the Lord. He should receive the glory in all our lives, but how much more in the work we do for His kingdom? So, when the enemy comes in like a flood, and the seeds of doubt are placed in your mind, just take time to stop and think about what we are doing here. We are working to see souls brought into the kingdom of God, to see believers walk in the victory that the Lord has provided, and experience the presence of God.

The Lord chooses imperfect people to carry out His perfect plan. So, when it seems like the task can't be done, or the coworker is too much to bear, remember that the Lord has placed us here for His plan and purpose. We never know when one decision that requires our attention will change the very course of a service, a share-a-thon, and the hearts and lives of those watching from afar.

We have a tremendous group of employees at Jimmy Swaggart Ministries. It's an honor and a privilege to work alongside each and every one of you. Let's keep working together to carry out the mission that the Lord has given all of us.

CHRISTLIKE UNITY

During a different share-a-thon, one of our newer employees (unbeknownst to me) sent this email:

As I am here translating and the Spirit of the Lord is moving and Donnie is asking first-time callers to come forward, I feel in my spirit that as employees of the ministry, we should also come forward and send the message that 'we are committed with the ministry to bringing the gospel to the world' and give in this share-a-thon $100 each.

So, I have taken the liberty of sending this email to challenge all to give $100. The ministry employs 205 of us. If we all give $100, our total donation will be $20,500. I hope you can be a part and if you can't give $100, do the best you can. God bless. Love Jesus out loud.

You see, there is an immense difference between the type of unity promoted at the Tucson memorial service and the type of unity promoted among our employees here at the ministry. The unity among us here (and among any true workers for God) is to promote one message, one truth, one Spirit, and one Lord — the Lord Jesus Christ!

At the Tucson service, the type of unity promoted would include any and every false god, spirit, and idol of all ages.

"Be you not unequally yoked together with unbelievers: for what fellowship hath righteousness with unrighteousness? and what communion hath light with darkness?" (II Cor. 6:14).

AND SARAH SAW

CHAPTER 22

WHO HAS BEWITCHED YOU?

WHO HAS BEWITCHED YOU?

WHERE IS BOASTING THEN? It is excluded. By what law? of works? No: but by the law of faith. Therefore we conclude that a man is justified by faith without the deeds of the law (Rom. 3:27-28).

I marvel that you are so soon removed from Him who called you into the grace of Christ unto another gospel (Gal. 1:6).

FREE FROM THE LAW!

Jesus has made us free from the law. The only governing principle of true Christianity is grace, which functions by faith. It is faith in Christ and what He did at Calvary alone that brings salvation, sanctification, and all other blessings and gifts of the Lord.

"For sin shall not have dominion over you: for you are not under the Law, but under Grace" (Rom. 6:14).

Thankfully, many Christians have been taught correctly in the sense of knowing that keeping a set of rules and regulations (including religious rituals and ceremonies) is not the means of being in right relationship with God. They know that such religiosity, in fact, makes void the finished work of Christ.

So, the Devil had to come up with a different type of legalism. He would now spiritualize his tactics in order to ensnare believers and keep them from living in the freedom and grace of Christ.

Believers, you must remember that just as you are not bound by physical or moral law-keeping — no matter how good the law may be — you are not bound by so-called universal "spiritual" laws either.

Jesus has made you free — free to place all your trust in what He did for you rather than your own moral or spiritual performance. The Christian life is lived out by faith in a work already finished.

THE RESULT OF SAVING FAITH

Trying to earn God's favor through any kind of law-keeping is considered empty works in the eyes of the Lord, which cannot redeem nor bring victory. Of course, when a believer truly lives in the grace afforded by Calvary, proper works, behaviors, actions, etc. will be the natural result, but works in and of themselves merit nothing. Good works are not the beginning of saving faith; they are the *result* of saving faith.

Believer, you have a choice to make. You can either trust in "words of faith" or the Word of Faith — Christ and Him

Crucified! But choose wisely because life will be found only in the latter.

"In the beginning was the Word, and the Word was with God, and the Word was God. The same was in the beginning with God. All things were made by Him; and without Him was not anything made that was made. In Him was Life; and the Life was the Light of men" (Jn. 1:1-4).

In reality, what has happened in the Word of Faith movement is that the words of Scripture have been turned into an idol, placed on a level above the God of the Scripture.

My husband said, "In practice, only certain Scriptures are used by the hyper-faith teachers to support their contentions. Their basic difficulty with the Word of God is that they separate the Word of God from the person of the Lord Jesus Christ. In short, they have replaced God with their chosen Scriptures, rationalizing that this will justify their actions. The words of Scripture are deified — apart from the living God — and exalted into various 'laws' which bring the forces of good and evil into action."

A Word of Faith legalism also makes it easy for people to become paranoid and obsessive. Some are taught that speaking information aloud allows the Devil to use that information to bring harm to them. They begin to fiercely guard every word uttered from their own mouths and often resort to policing the mouths of others. They are literally afraid of the words they speak.

"For God hath not given us the spirit of fear; but of power, and of love, and of a sound mind" (II Tim. 1:7).

Practitioners also soon come to realize that it is impossible to escape the plague of guilt that accompanies the inevitable failure to perfectly adhere to spiritual laws. They are left thinking that the pain and suffering in their lives and in the lives of their loved ones is their fault, solely due to things they failed to believe or speak correctly.

For instance, according to the "law of attraction," no mother should ever think, "I'm afraid my son will be killed in Iraq." Although it's an honest expression of emotion regarding a real threat, she may fear that just by worrying about it she has somehow summoned the universe to cause that exact thing to happen.

After all, *The Secret* teaches: "Whatever is going on in your mind is what you are attracting ... We are like magnets — like attract like. You become and attract what you think ... Every thought has a frequency. Thoughts send out a magnetic energy ... What you focus on with your thought and feeling is what you attract into your experience ... Those who speak most of illness have illness, those who speak most of prosperity have it."

What a horribly abusive idea to perpetuate, as if the so-called power of subconscious thoughts could bring harm to another. Again, these spiritual laws do not bring freedom; they bring fear. Legalism, even when practiced only in the mind, is bondage.

"Stand fast therefore in the liberty wherewith Christ has made us free, and be not entangled again with the yoke of bondage" (Gal. 5:1).

SUPERSTITION

In fact, the spiritual laws presented by the Devil (whether inside the church as the Word of Faith teachings or in the secular world as the mind science teachings) lead to nothing but superstition in the lives of those who try to live by them.

One dictionary defines superstition as "an irrational belief that an object, action, or circumstance not logically related to a course of events influences its outcome."

Behavioral psychologist, B. F. Skinner, claims to have demonstrated how superstitious behavior can be created as a result of "coincidental" or "accidental" reinforcement.

In an experiment using pigeons, Skinner released pellets of food into a box at fixed interval time periods. Although the release of food had nothing to do with the behavior of the pigeons, the pigeons tended to increase and repeat whatever specific behaviors they had done just prior to the last release of food (behaviors such as turning in circles, nodding the head up and down, or picking up one foot).

The behavior of the pigeons was "accidentally" reinforced, so they developed ritualistic behavior in their desire for more food. This happens often when people try to keep mystic laws. They misinterpret good events in their lives as having resulted from their keeping of these laws, when the two do not actually have a causal relationship.

And being a master psychologist himself, the Devil will make sure "accidental" reinforcement occurs. This is one way he crafts false signs that lead people astray. *"Even him, whose coming is after the working of Satan with all power and signs and lying wonders"* (II Thess. 2:9).

A Believer must never resort to seeking after signs; he must always seek the truth of Jesus Christ.

THE SIN OF LYING?

Another definition of superstition: "A notion maintained despite evidence to the contrary." This is glaringly obvious with the "power of the spoken word" or Word of Faith doctrines.

We have people running around confessing things that are simply not true because, remember, no one is ever to confess anything negative. Whatever happened to the sin of lying? If the Word of Faith doctrine was truly of God, it would not be causing people to sin.

The Devil, however, will always try to get people wrapped up in sin, purposely trying to drive a wedge between them and the Lord. Some will claim perfect health when they cannot even get out of bed, because their superstitious law tells them that admitting their sickness will doom them to additional sickness. Many will refuse to go to a doctor.

One ministry states: "Christian Science makes sickness an illusion and one overcomes it with correct thinking, it is the same thing in the word of faith movement, they believe their body is lying to them. They disbelieve the symptoms, and stand on continual positive confession of the word to relieve themselves."

Another huge evidence to the contrary regarding the

validity of these ancient occult spiritual laws is that, in the lives of most practitioners, it just hasn't worked.

Do you see the millions of people now learning the techniques of *The Secret* and the "law of attraction" all becoming millionaires? Do you see entire congregations in Word of Faith churches becoming millionaires? No, and you never will.

The only people getting rich are the so-called preachers, motivational speakers, or New Age gurus who sell you the books, tapes, seminars, etc., which teach these lies in the first place. Just follow the money trail to see who is really being "blessed."

Of course, as we have also previously discussed, Word of Faith teachers will try to use Scripture to justify these perversities, but the true meaning of the Scripture used is always something entirely different.

Proverbs 23:7 is one example. It says, *"For as he thinks in his heart, so is he."*

This does not mean that a man's thoughts determine his life. In the correct context, this verse is referring to a deceitful man who may pretend to be your friend for social or religious purposes, but in the end, he is not a genuine friend to any man, because his heart is selfish.

Here are some other verses that Word of Faith preachers commonly misuse: *"Keep your tongue from evil, and your lips from speaking guile"* (Ps. 34:13).

"Death and life are in the power of the tongue: and they who love it shall eat the fruit thereof" (Prov. 18:21).

These verses do not mean that we create our own realities through the words we speak, as faith teachers would like us to believe. They are referring to a properly disciplined tongue, which will not become the cause of heartache in the lives of those around us. Do not be deceived when Bible verses are taken out of context and twisted to fit occult doctrines. Look at the overall message of the passage.

And, just to keep us all in check, neither is the Message of the Cross a magic talisman one may confess to invoke the power of God. Just because we know the right message doesn't mean that we are immune from using it improperly (or super-stitiously), just as the Word of Faith camp misuses Scripture.

Yes, everything we will ever need comes from the Cross, but this great gospel message is meant to be our entire faith for living, not a positive confession to obtain every little thing we desire. God is not fooled by our religious tricks and manipulations of Him. He knows what the Message of the Cross truly means in each and every one of our lives. He sees whether we want to use faith for temporal gain or if we have truly surrendered our will to His.

Also, remember that just as occult spiritual laws create irrational superstition, they will also continue to lead one fur-ther and further away from all logic, eventually reaching the spirit realm of the demonic.

The Bible warns us of being "bewitched," which has the im-plication of being charmed or put under a spell — again, being void of logical thinking. The believers in Galatia were led astray from the truth due to a lack of sound and rational judgment.

"O foolish Galatians, who has bewitched you, that you should not obey the truth, before whose eyes Jesus Christ has been evidently set forth, crucified among you?" (Gal. 3:1).

Remember that Ester Hicks, teacher of the universal "law of attraction," said that she began channeling a collective spirit that she called "Abraham." "I just relax and quiet my mind," she said.

You see, learning the 'spiritual laws' is only the first step. You will later be enticed with meditative practices that are said to improve the keeping of these laws. But, this is exactly what brought Hicks into contact with her spirit guide. What she described was actually a deep meditative state, which is a state of self-hypnosis or trance where the subconscious mind is exposed. It is what some call going into "the silence," "the stillness," or "the center."

As a matter of fact, meditation is swiftly becoming the main vehicle for creating a worldwide acceptance of the universal spirituality of the Antichrist. Spirits contacted during meditation will impress upon the practitioner the beliefs of esoteric theosophy and the New Age, not the beliefs of orthodox Christianity.

As believers, we must be increasingly discerning in these last days.

AND SARAH SAW

CHAPTER 23

THE RAPTURE OF
THE CHURCH

THE RAPTURE OF THE CHURCH

THE NEXT MAJOR BIBLICAL event in history will be the rapture of the church. Are you watching? Are you ready?

We believe in and teach a pre-tribulation rapture, meaning that the rapture will take place before the great tribulation and could occur at any moment. The most vivid description of the rapture of the church is given in Paul's first epistle to the Thessalonians:

"For the Lord Himself shall descend from heaven with a shout, with the voice of the archangel, and with the trump of God: and the dead in Christ shall rise first: Then we who are alive and remain shall be caught up together with them in the clouds, to meet the Lord in the air: and so shall we ever be with the Lord" (I Thess. 4:16-17).

The word *rapture* is actually the one-word synonym that believers use in place of the phrase "caught up." In the original Greek text, the word used is *harpazo,* meaning to "to seize upon by force," "to snatch up." It was actually Latin translators who chose the word *rapture,* from the term *raptus,* meaning "to seize." It can imply a sudden, swift occurrence.

Rapture is also defined as the transporting of a person from one place to another, such as from earth to heaven, or the changing of a person from one state to another, such as from a physical body to a spirit body.

RAPTURE!

Now, in an effort to cast doubt upon this soon-coming event, some have attempted to claim that rapture is not a biblical term and, therefore, not a valid part of Bible prophecy. Truthfully though, it is just as biblical as the words *God* or *Jesus*.

Almost all words in our English Bible are translations of Greek and Hebrew expressions, none of which were originally found in the form that we have come to know them today. *God* is a proper and meaningful translation of certain words in the original languages, and *Jesus* is a good translation for His name, *Yeshua* (*Joshua*), meaning "the Lord saves" in Hebrew.

Likewise, the English word *rapture*, which means "to be caught up," is an excellent translation for the Greek word *harpazo*. Paul referred to the rapture as the "blessed hope" of the church: *"Looking for that blessed hope, and the glorious appearing of the great God and our Saviour Jesus Christ"* (Titus 2:13).

The purpose of the rapture will be to resurrect all of the righteous dead from each dispensation and reunite the soul and spirit with a new glorified body (I Cor. 15:35-55).

Actually, "the resurrection of the saints" is another phrase believers have used through the years to describe this promised event. The righteous dead will be caught up, along with all the saints still living on the earth, to meet the Lord in the air and return with Him to heaven (Jn. 14:1-3). The glorified bodies we will receive will be spirit, empowered by the Holy Spirit, rather than physical.

PRE-TRIBULATION RAPTURE

As previously mentioned, we believe that the Bible teaches the rapture will occur before the great tribulation:

"Because you have kept the word of My patience, I also will keep you from the hour of temptation (the great tribulation)*, which shall come upon all the world, to try them that dwell upon the earth"* (Rev. 3:10).

Several more Scriptures attest to a pre-tribulation rapture:

Luke 21:36: *"Watch you therefore, and pray always, that you may be accounted worthy to escape all these things* (the tribulation) *that shall come to pass, and to stand before the Son of Man."*

I Thessalonians 5:9: *"For God has not appointed us to wrath* (the tribulation)*, but to obtain salvation by our Lord Jesus Christ."*

II Thessalonians 2:7-8: *"The mystery of iniquity does already work: only he* (the church) *who now lets will let, until he be taken out of the way. And then shall that Wicked be revealed."*

Revelation 4:1: *"After this I looked, and, behold, a door was opened in heaven: and the first voice which I heard was as it were of a trumpet talking with me; which said, Come up hither, and I will show you things which must be hereafter* (after the rapture of the church)."

The above Scriptures, and plenty of others also, demonstrate that even the New Testament saints were looking for the rapture — or resurrection — to occur, so how much closer are we today? To further clarify, we believe the sequence of these coming end-time events will be: first, the rapture; second, the great tribulation; and then, the Lord's return (the second coming).

CALVARY

Now, this is not to say that prior to the rapture, the church will not experience persecution as the world becomes more and more wicked, but the great tribulation is really about God's judgment upon sin. And, for believers, God's judgment was already poured out at Calvary. Christ bore our sins in His body on the Cross not to be brought to our account again. They have been forgiven and forgotten (Isa. 43:25; I Pet. 2:24). Thank you, Jesus!

So, while the earth and those still upon it are going through the great tribulation, the raptured saints of God will be simultaneously attending events in heaven — namely, the judgment seat of Christ (Rom. 14:10; II Cor. 5:10) and the marriage supper of the Lamb (Mat. 26:29; Rev. 19:7-9).

In the book of Revelation, note is made of those who *"dwell in heaven"* and those who *"dwell on earth."* The former group, the church, will have been given our resurrection bodies and will walk in the company of the Lamb and His holy angels in heaven. The latter, those dwelling on earth, include non-believers, God's 144,000 Jewish evangelists (regenerated men who do not yet have resurrection bodies), and their converts (the tribulation saints). Many of these new saints will become martyrs during the tribulation, but they will not be given their resurrection bodies until the tribulation ends (Rev. 20:4).

THE RAPTURE AND THE SECOND COMING

Many people fail to distinguish between the rapture of the church and the second coming of Christ. Here are lists describing each:

The rapture of the church:
1. Occurs *before* the tribulation (Lk. 21:36)
2. Christ comes *for* the saints (I Thess. 4:13-17)
3. Christ takes the saints to *heaven* (Jn. 14:3)
4. Christ returns to the *clouds* (I Thess. 4:17)
5. Christ is not seen (I Cor. 15:52).

The second coming of Christ:

1. Occurs *after* the tribulation (Mat. 24:29-30)
2. Christ comes *with* the saints (Jude 14; Rev. 19:11-21)
3. Christ brings the saints back to *earth* (Zech. 14:4-5; Rev. 19:14)

4. Christ returns to the *earth* (Zech. 14:4-5)
5. Every eye shall see Christ (Rev. 1:7)
6. It is the great day of His *"wrath"* (Rev. 19:15)

ISRAEL

Only one archangel, Michael, is called by name in Scripture, and his specific jurisdiction is over the people of Israel. At the time of the rapture, he will signal to Israel that God has at last returned His focus to the final redemption of His chosen nation.

This event was spoken of by Daniel: *"And at that time shall Michael stand up, the great prince which stands for the children of your people: and there shall be a time of trouble, such as never was since there was a nation even to that same time: and at that time your people shall be delivered, every one who shall be found written in the book"* (Dan. 12:1).

The phrase, *"A time of trouble, such as never was since there was a nation even to that same time,"* is the same thing Jesus would later say. It concerns the last three and a half years of the tribulation.

Matthew 24:21 states: *"For then shall be great tribulation, such as was not since the beginning of the world to this time, no, nor ever shall be."*

This will be the worst tribulation the world has ever known — so bad that it will never again be repeated.

Matthew 24:22 states: *"And except those days should be shortened, there should no flesh be saved: but for the elect's sake those days shall be shortened."*

Israel will come close to extinction, but God's love for His people will cause Him to shorten the days with the second coming of the Lord. In Matthew 24:27-31, we read:

> *"For as the lightning cometh out of the east, and shineth even unto the west; so shall also the coming of the Son of Man be. For wheresoever the carcass is, there will the eagles be gathered together. Immediately after the tribulation of those days shall the sun be darkened, and the moon shall not give her light, and the stars shall fall from heaven, and the powers of the heavens shall be shaken: And then shall appear the sign of the Son of Man in heaven: and then shall all the tribes of the earth mourn, and they shall see the Son of Man coming in the clouds of heaven with power and great glory. And He shall send His angels with a great sound of a trumpet, and they shall gather together His elect from the four winds, from one end of heaven to the other."*

So, at the time that Jesus calls His church out of the world (the rapture of the church and not the second coming), three specific events take place:

1. The call of command from the lips of Jesus to awaken the dead in Christ and bring them forth from their graves, just as Jesus called His friend Lazarus forth (Jn. 11:43).
2. The archangel's call to Israel that God's focus has returned to Israel (Dan. 12:1).

3. The trumpet call (not to be confused with the last seven trumpets in Revelation) is a trumpet call associated with the Jewish Feast of Tabernacles and will be used to call the living saints at the time of the rapture. This is described in I Corinthians 15:50-58:

    'Now this I say, brethren, that flesh and blood cannot inherit the kingdom of God; neither does corruption inherit incorruption. Behold, I show you a mystery; We shall not all sleep, but we shall all be changed, In a moment, in the twinkling of an eye, at the last trump: for the trumpet shall sound, and the dead shall be raised incorruptible, and we shall be changed. For this corruptible must put on incorruption, and this mortal must put on immortality. So when this corruptible shall have put on incorruption, and this mortal shall have put on immortality, then shall be brought to pass the saying that is written, Death is swallowed up in victory. O death, where is your sting? O grave, where is your victory? The sting of death is sin; and the strength of sin is the law. But thanks be to God, which gives us the victory through our Lord Jesus Christ. Therefore, my beloved brethren, be ye stedfast, unmoveable, always abounding in the work of the Lord, forasmuch as you know that your labour is not in vain in the Lord.'

NO MORE MORTALITY, NO MORE SIN NATURE

Praise God, the rapture will bring the completed

manifestation of Christ's finished work for us at Calvary! For the believer, the rapture is independence day! Once and for all, we will be totally and completely freed from our corrupted nature, freed from all effects of sin! Glory to God!

Let's take a closer look at the events taking place in heaven (which parallel the events of the tribulation on earth). All believers must appear before the judgment seat of Christ according to II Corinthians 5:10.

Remember this is not for the purpose of dealing with sin; however, a careful ledger has been kept of every work the believer has performed since he became a Christian (Mat. 12:36; Rom. 14:12; II Cor. 5:10).

Believers will be judged on the basis of:

1. Doctrinal beliefs — true or false (Rom. 2:14-16; 14:1-10).
2. Conduct toward others — kind or unkind (Mat. 18:10; Mk. 9:41; II Tim. 4:14).
3. Stewardship — faithful or unfaithful (Mat. 25:14-29; Lk. 12:42-44; I Cor. 4:1-5).
4. Words — good or bad (Mat. 12:36-37; Eph. 4:29).
5. Talents — used or wasted (Mat. 5:15-16; Mk. 4:25).
6. Attitudes — Christlike or selfish (Mat. 6:1-7; Eph. 4:30-32).
7. Motives — right or wrong (Mat. 6:16-18; Lk. 14:12-14).
8. Traits — Spiritual or carnal (Rom. 2:1-6; Col. 3:8-16).
9. Every deed — worthy or worthless (Mk. 9:41; Col. 3:23-25).

The deeds performed in a worthy manner will be rewarded, but those deeds Christ judges unworthy will be burned and will cause the believer lost rewards (I Cor. 3:12-15).

The following rewards have been promised for faithful service to the Lord:

1. Victor's crown (I Cor. 9:25)
2. Crown of righteousness (II Tim. 4:8)
3. Crown of rejoicing (I Thess. 2:19)
4. Crown of life (James 1:12)
5. Crown of glory (I Pet. 5:4)
6. Martyr's crown (Rev. 2:10)
7. Crown of gold (Rev. 4:4)

Because Scripture clearly indicates that it is possible for someone else to take our crown (Rev. 3:11), it behooves every Christian to be diligent in his service to the King of kings.

Believers will also be given a mansion in which to live eternally (Jn. 14:2), and Christ will determine the amount of earthly rulership to give each saint based on his faithfulness to God in this present life (Lk. 19:12-26).

Believers will reign as kings and priests with Christ forever (Rev. 1:6; 5:10).

Following the judgment seat of Christ will be the marriage supper of the Lamb. This speaks of the bride of Christ, all the redeemed from every dispensation who will live in the New Jerusalem.

"Let us be glad and rejoice, and give honour to Him: for the marriage of the Lamb is come, and His wife has made herself ready. And to her was granted that she should be

arrayed in fine linen, clean and white: for the fine linen is the righteousness of saints. And he said unto me, Write, Blessed are they which are called unto the marriage supper of the Lamb. And he said unto me, These are the true sayings of God" (Rev. 19:7-9).

What a time of reunion, celebration, and worship believers have in store! Are you ready? Are you in a committed, covenant relationship with Christ? Are you a bride adorned for her husband? Is your heart singing, *"When I hear that last trumpet sound, my feet won't stay on the ground"*? If your answers are yes, then, as my husband often says, "Well, glory!"

AND SARAH SAW

CHAPTER 24

CHRIST CRUCIFIED
BY J.C. RYLE

CHRIST CRUCIFIED
BY J. C. RYLE

THE TEXT OF THIS sermon was sent to me by one of our SBN listeners. As I read it, I was so blessed that I wanted to share it with all of you. It was written in the 1800s by J. C. Ryle, the first Anglican bishop of Liverpool, England.

Bishop Ryle was born at Park House, Macclesfield, in 1816 to parents John and Susannah Ryle who made their fortune in the silk mills during the Industrial Revolution. Their wealth afforded Ryle an education at Eton College and Christ Church, Oxford, and supported his ambitions to take up a career in politics at Parliament.

However, after suffering an illness and watching his father face sudden bankruptcy, Ryle turned to the church for comfort. After hearing Ephesians 2:8-9 read aloud in the service, the 22-year-old experienced a spiritual awakening and decided to become a minister. Four years later, Ryle was ordained by Bishop C. R. Sumner at Winchester. As a parish priest, Ryle would spend the next 38 years serving congregations at Helmingham, Suffolk, and Stradbroke.

His roles in the church as rector and vicar eventually led

to a position as honorary canon in Norwich and a tenure as Dean of Salisbury. Throughout his career, Ryle built more than 40 churches and created a pension fund for the clergy of his diocese.

At the age of 64, Ryle was appointed to be the new see of Liverpool on the recommendation of Prime Minister Benjamin Disraeli and served in this position until his retirement in 1900, the same year of his death. The text of his sermon follows.

CHRIST CRUCIFIED

There is no doctrine in Christianity so important as the doctrine of Christ crucified. There is none in which the Devil tries so hard to destroy. There is none that it is so needful for our own peace to understand.

By 'Christ crucified,' I mean the doctrine that Christ suffered death on the Cross to make atonement for our sins, that by His death He made a full, perfect, and complete satisfaction to God for the ungodly, and that through the merits of that death, *all who believe in Him* are forgiven all their sins, however many and great, entirely, and forever. About this blessed doctrine, let me say a few words.

The doctrine of Christ crucified is the *grand peculiarity of the Christian religion*. Other religions have laws and moral precepts, forms and ceremonies, rewards and punishments; but other religions cannot tell us of a dying Saviour: they cannot show us the cross. This is the crown and glory of

CHAPTER TWENTY-FOUR | **309**

the gospel; this is that special comfort which belongs to it alone. Miserable indeed is that religious teaching which calls itself Christian, and yet contains nothing of the cross. A man who teaches in this way might as well profess to explain the solar system, and yet tell his hearers nothing about the sun.

The doctrine of Christ crucified *is the strength of a minister*. I for one would not be without it for all the world. I should feel like a soldier without arms, like an artist without his pencil, like a pilot without his compass, like a labourer without his tools. Let others, if they will, preach the law and morality; let others hold forth the terrors of hell and the joys of heaven; let others dwell on the sacraments and the church: give me the Cross of Christ. This is the only lever which has ever turned the world upside down hitherto and made men forsake their sins: and if this will not, nothing will.

A man may begin preaching with a perfect knowledge of Latin, Greek, and Hebrew, but he will do little or no good among his hearers unless he knows something of the Cross. Never was there a minister who did much for the conversion of souls who did not dwell much on Christ crucified. Luther, Rutherford, Whitfield, M'Cheyne, were all most eminently preachers of the Cross. This is the preaching that the Holy Ghost delights to bless: He loves to honour those who honour the Cross.

The doctrine of Christ crucified is *the secret of all*

missionary success. Nothing but this has ever moved the hearts of the heathen. Just according as this has been lifted up, missions have prospered. This is the weapon that has won victories over hearts of every kind, in every quarter of the globe: Greenlanders, Africans, South Sea Islanders, Hindus, and Chinese, all have alike felt its power. Just as that huge iron tube which crosses the Menai Straits is more affected and bent by half an hour's sunshine than by all the dead weight that can be placed in it, so in like manner the hearts of savages have melted before the Cross, when every other argument seemed to move them no more than stones.

'Brethren,' said a North American Indian after his conversion, 'I have been a heathen. I know how heathens think. Once a preacher came and began to explain to us that there was a God, but we told him to return to the place from whence he came. Another preacher came and told us not to lie, nor steal, nor drink, but we did not heed him. At last another came into my hut one day and said, "I am come to you in the name of the Lord of heaven and earth. He sends to let you know that He will make you happy and deliver you from misery. For this end He became a man, gave His life a ransom, and shed His blood for sinners." I could not forget his words. I told them to the other Indians, and an awakening began among us. I say, therefore, preach the sufferings and death of Christ, our Saviour, if you wish your words to gain entrance among the heathen.'

Never indeed did the Devil triumph so thoroughly as when he persuaded the Jesuit missionaries in China to keep back the story of the Cross!

The doctrine of Christ crucified is *the foundation of a church's prosperity*. No church will ever be honoured in which Christ crucified is not continually lifted up. Nothing whatever can make up for the want of the Cross. Without it, all things may be done decently and in order; without it, there may be splendid ceremonies, beautiful music, gorgeous churches, learned ministers, crowded communion tables, huge collections for the poor; but without the Cross, no good will be done. Dark hearts will not be enlightened, proud hearts will not be humbled, mourning hearts will not be comforted, fainting hearts will not be cheered. Sermons about the Catholic Church and an apostolic ministry, sermons about baptism and the Lord's Supper, sermons about unity and schism, sermons about fasts and communion, sermons about fathers and saints, such sermons will never make up for the absence of sermons about the Cross of Christ. They may amuse some, *they will feed none*.

A gorgeous banqueting room and splendid gold plates on the table will never make up to a hungry man for the want of food. Christ crucified is God's grand ordinance for doing good to men. Whenever a church keeps back Christ crucified or puts anything whatever in that foremost place which Christ crucified should always have, from that moment a church ceases to be useful. Without

Christ crucified in her pulpits, a church is little better than a cumberer of the ground, a dead carcass, a well without water, a barren fig tree, a sleeping watchman, a silent trumpet, a dumb witness, an ambassador without terms of peace, a messenger without tidings, a lighthouse without fire, a stumblingblock to weak believers, a comfort to infidels, a hot bed for formalism, a joy to the Devil, and an offence to God.

The doctrine of Christ crucified is *the grand centre of union* among true Christians. Our outward differences are many without doubt: one man is an Episcopalian, another is a Presbyterian; one is an Independent, another a Baptist; one is a Calvinist, another an Arminian; one is a Lutheran, another a Plymouth Brother; one is a friend to establishments, another a friend to the voluntary system; one is a friend to liturgies, another a friend to extempore prayer: but after all, what shall we hear about most of these differences in heaven? Nothing, most probably: nothing at all.

Does a man really and sincerely glory in the Cross of Christ? That is the grand question. If he does, he is my brother: we are traveling on the same road; we are journeying towards a home where Christ is all, and everything outward in religion will be forgotten. But if he does not glory in the Cross of Christ, I cannot feel comfort about him. Union on outward points only is union only for time: union about the Cross is union for eternity. Error on outward points is only a skin-deep disease: error about the Cross is disease at the heart. Union about outward points is a mere man-made union: union about the Cross of Christ can only be produced by the Holy Ghost.

Reader, I know not what you think of all this. I feel as if the half of what I desire to tell you about Christ crucified was left untold. But I do hope that I have given you something to think about. Listen to me now for a few moments while I say something to apply the whole subject to your conscience.

Are you living in any kind of sin? Are you following the course of this world and neglecting your soul? Hear, I beseech you, what I say to you this day: Behold the Cross of Christ! See there how Jesus loved you! See there what Jesus suffered to prepare for you a way of salvation! Yes: careless men and women, for you that blood was shed! For you those hands and feet were pierced with nails! For you that body hung in agony on the Cross! You are they whom Jesus loved, and for whom He died! Surely that love ought to melt you: surely the thought of the Cross should draw you to repentance. Oh, that it might be so this very day! Oh, that you would come at once to that Saviour who died for you and is willing to save! Come and cry to Him with the prayer of faith, and I know that He will listen. Come and lay hold upon the Cross, and I know that He will not cast you out. Come and believe on Him who died on the Cross, and this very day you shall have eternal life.

Are you inquiring the way toward heaven? Are you seeking salvation but doubtful whether you can find it? Are you desiring to have an interest in Christ but doubting whether Christ will receive you? To you also I say this day, 'Behold the Cross of Christ.' Here is encouragement if you really want it. Draw near to the Lord Jesus with boldness, for nothing need keep you back: His arms are open to receive you; His heart is full of love towards you. He has made a way by which you may approach Him with confidence. Think of the Cross. Draw near and fear not.

Are you an unlearned man? Are you desirous to get to heaven, and yet perplexed and brought to a standstill by difficulties in the Bible that you cannot explain? To you also I say this day, 'Behold the Cross of Christ.' Read there the Father's love and the Son's compassion. Surely they are written in great plain letters, which none can well mistake. What, though, you are now perplexed by the doctrine of election? What, though, at present you cannot reconcile your own utter corruption and your own responsibility? Look, I say, at the Cross. Does not that Cross tell you that Jesus is a mighty, loving, and ready Saviour? Does it not make one thing plain, and that is that if not saved, it is all your own fault? Oh, get hold of that truth and hold it fast!

Are you a distressed believer? Is your heart pressed down with sickness, tried with disappointments, overburdened with cares? To you also I say this day, 'Behold the Cross of Christ.' Think whose hand it is that chastens you: think whose hand is measuring to you the cup of bitterness which you are now drinking. It is the hand of Him that was crucified: it is the same hand that in love to your soul was nailed to the accursed tree. Surely that thought should comfort and hearten you. Surely you should say to yourself, 'A crucified Saviour will never lay upon me anything that is not good for me. There is a needs be. It must be well.'

Are you a dying believer? Have you gone to that bed from which something within tells you you will never come down alive? Are you drawing near to that solemn hour when soul and body must part for a season, and you must launch into a world unknown? Oh, look steadily at the Cross of Christ, and you shall be kept in peace! Fix the eyes of your mind firmly on Jesus crucified, and He shall deliver you from all your fears. Though you walk through dark places, He will be with you: He will never leave you, never forsake you. Sit under the shadow of the Cross to the very last, and its fruits shall be sweet to your taste. There is but one thing needful on a deathbed, and that is to feel one's arms around the Cross.

Reader, if you never heard of Christ crucified before this day, I can wish you nothing better than that you may know Him by faith and rest on Him for salvation. If you do know Him, may you know Him better every year you live till you see Him face to face.

AND SARAH SAW

CHAPTER 25

THE MESSAGE OF
THE CROSS

THE MESSAGE OF THE CROSS

RECENTLY, I WAS ASKED if we could reprint my husband's article, "The Vision Of Daniel," from a former issue of *The Evangelist*, which included a section titled, "The Cross Of Christ, The Last Great Push By The Holy Spirit."

He was sharing with the people the revelation of the Cross that was given to him by God, as well as another word from the Lord given to him in 1992. It seems that some are misrepresenting what was contained in that article; therefore, we felt it would be good to offer it to you again.

When my husband used the word *revelation,* some thought he was meaning a revelation outside of Scripture. Of course, this accusation is false. In his article, he states, "When the revelation began to come, which, in effect, was not at all new, but rather was that which was originally given to the Apostle Paul, it totally revolutionized my life."

He states a few sentences later, "In this revelation, the Lord explained to me, even in graphic detail, that which He had originally given to the Apostle Paul (Gal 1:12). But I honestly think, in His explaining this revelation to me, that

He gave me more light than the church has previously known as it regards this all-important subject."

Notice he states that the Lord gave him "more light than the church" had previously known; he does not say that the Lord gave him more light than Paul had known or more light than God had given to Paul.

THE CHURCH

The indictment is against the church, not Paul or the Bible. He was putting the blame on the church world as a whole, including himself, for our inadequacy in understanding the fullness of the Message of the Cross. There was in no way any indication that God had not done His part by leaving something out of His Word or that this revelation was given to my husband exclusively.

Anyone who has listened to my husband for any length of time knows that he would never even indicate, much less state, that the Word of God is by any means imperfect or incomplete. Also, he would never insinuate that God's truth was not readily available to any and all individuals who study His Word. This is not part of who he is. My husband has made it his life's work to study the Bible because he knows that in it, God has *"given unto us all things that pertain unto life and godliness"* (II Pet 1:3).

This revelation of the Cross was expressly written in the Bible, and copious verses of Scripture both confirm and substantiate it.

REVELATION

When you look up the word *revelation* in the dictionary, it can be described as "an act of revealing or communicating divine truth or an enlightening or astonishing disclosure." Another dictionary I looked at used the word *illumination.*

Now, I'm sure that all of you who read your Bible have had a verse or passage of Scripture just suddenly seem to jump off the page as you read it, and you felt as if you were seeing it or better understanding it much more than ever before. You may have read that verse a thousand times, yet it had never fully sunk in until it was illuminated or revealed to you by the Spirit of God in a special, personal way. Some have called this experiencing a "rhema" word from God. It is as if you hear the voice of God in your spirit (although not in an audible voice) teaching His Word to you.

It's seriously sad to have to say that some wannabe apologists have written blogs or articles accusing my husband of saying that he "was given a revelation greater than Paul's." As we have just explained, this was just not correct.

No, my husband has not said that this revelation of the new covenant was greater than Paul's. And no, his revelation is not separate from the Bible. Unfortunately, when you begin to explain to someone, particularly a church leader, that there has been something in Scripture he previously did not understand to its full extent, it often insults his pride, especially if he doesn't want to accept the truth that's being accentuated by the Holy Spirit. Most do not take correction well, and if you accept the scriptural revelation of the Cross, you may have to accept the need for changes in your church programs, teachings, and activities. The Cross is the only way for both salvation and sanctification, and any church activity that doesn't strictly adhere to it must go.

In these last days, we true Christians know all too well that the enemy is working overtime to discredit the things of God and those working for Him. I consider it a privilege to have this opportunity to expose his evil activities by emphasizing this important teaching in my husband's article, in his own words, provided below for to you to read for yourself.

THE CROSS OF CHRIST, THE LAST GREAT PUSH BY THE HOLY SPIRIT

I am going to divulge something that I believe the Lord gave to me in 1992, to which I have seldom alluded.

It was either late winter or early spring when a few of us had gathered for prayer at 10 a.m. that particular day, which was our custom. The Spirit of the Lord was to move in a tremendous way in that prayer meeting.

I was seeking the Lord for help as it regarded my own person and this ministry, and was being greatly moved upon by the Holy Spirit to intercede on behalf of specific needs.

Realizing, and graphically seeing my own shortcomings and crying to the Lord for help, the Lord spoke to me.

He spoke graphically to my heart, certainly acknowledging

my personal needs, to which I will direct more attention in a moment; but then, He began to speak to me as it regarded the church world as a whole.

To do so, He took me to the statements of the prophet Isaiah. The prophet said:

Ah sinful nation, a people laden with iniquity, a seed of evildoers, children who are corrupters: they have forsaken the LORD, *they have provoked the Holy One of Israel unto anger, they are gone away backward. Why should you be stricken any more? you will revolt more and more: the whole head is sick, and the whole heart faint. From the sole of the foot even unto the head there is no soundness in it; but wounds, and bruises, and putrifying sores: they* (the sores) *have not been closed, neither bound up, neither mollified with ointment* (Isa. 1:4-6).

The Lord was telling me that not only did I need help, but, as well, the entirety of the church world fell into the same category.

As stated, this was in 1992, approximately five years before the Lord would give to me the revelation of the Cross. When that revelation began to come, which, in effect, was not at all new, but rather, was that which was originally given to the Apostle Paul, it totally revolutionized my life. In this revelation, the Lord explained to me, even in graphic detail, that which He had originally given to the apostle Paul (Gal. 1:12).

But I honestly think that in His explaining this revelation to me, He gave me more light than the church has previously known as it regards this all-important subject.

In effect, the revelation of the Cross, for that's what it was, is the understanding and explanation of the new covenant; therefore, one could say that the story of the new covenant is the story of the Cross. Consequently, it could also be said that the story of the Cross is the story of the new covenant.

THE HOLY SPIRIT

That which the Lord gave to me, which I believe sheds more light on what was originally given to Paul, pertains to the manner in which the Holy Spirit works within our hearts and lives.

To make it brief, the Lord Jesus Christ is the source of all that we receive from God, with the Cross being the means. It is this means in which the Holy Spirit works; in other words, the death of Christ on the Cross was a legal work, hence, it affording justification by faith (Rom. 5:1). The Holy Spirit works strictly within the legal parameters of this finished work.

In fact, He works so strictly within these legal parameters of the Cross that His work is referred to as *"the law of the Spirit of life in Christ Jesus"* (Rom. 8:2).

THE CROSS, OUR FAITH,
AND THE HOLY SPIRIT

Putting it all together, the Lord showed me, as stated, that the Cross is the means by which our Lord gives to us all things, and that He does this by and through the person, work, ministry, and office of the Holy Spirit (Jn. 16:7-15; Rom. 8:1-2, 11).

Every single thing done in our hearts and lives that is from the Lord is carried out completely by the Holy Spirit. As it regards the believer, we, within ourselves, have no power to change anything. It is the Holy Spirit who alone does the changing, and who does so by His mighty power.

That's the reason that Paul said, *"For the preaching of the Cross is to them who perish foolishness; but unto us who are saved it is the power of God"* (I Cor. 1:18).

The preaching of the Cross is the power of God because the Holy Spirit, who alone has the power, works exclusively within the parameters of the finished work of Christ. In other words, when the preacher preaches the Cross and the people believe what is being preached, this opens the door for the Holy Spirit to work mightily on our behalf.

He demands of us very few things, but He definitely does demand that we understand that Christ is the source, and the Cross is the means, and that we, at all times, place our faith and confidence in that finished work. Doing that, and

I speak of our faith ever having the Cross as its object, the Holy Spirit gives us the power to live a holy life. In fact, that's the only way that it can be accomplished (Gal. 2:20-21).

I have always preached the Cross; however, it was not until 1997 that I understood the Cross as it regards victorious living. To show me all of that, the Lord took me to Romans, Chapters 6, 7, and 8.

FALSE WAYS

I grieve when I see preachers promoting one scheme after the other, claiming that such will bring about victorious living. There's only one message that can bring about such victory, and it is Jesus Christ and Him crucified (I Cor. 1:23).

Sometime back, a preacher, with whom I was not acquainted, wrote me a lengthy letter, explaining one of these latest fads. I answered him by saying, "My brother, the answer for which you seek, and the only answer, is the Cross of Christ."

It is amazing that the modern church completely discounts sin, with many in its confines actually ignoring sin altogether as if it doesn't exist.

The truth is, as sin is the problem of the unredeemed, most definitely, it is also the problem of the redeemed.

Listen again to Paul: *For what the law* (law of Moses)

could not do, in that it was weak through the flesh (man, in his fallen condition, didn't have, and doesn't have, the ability within himself to properly obey the law), *God sending His own Son in the likeness of sinful flesh* (the incarnation, God becoming man; this doesn't say that the humanity of Christ was sinful, but rather that the humanity of our Lord was in the likeness of sinful flesh), *and for sin* (meaning that sin is the very purpose and reason that God became man, was born of the Virgin Mary, and went to the Cross), *condemned sin in the flesh* (meaning that Christ made it possible through the Cross for us to live a victorious, overcoming life) (Rom. 8:3).

SIN

In other words, the very reason that the Lord came to this world and went to the Cross, for that was ever His mission (I Pet. 1:18-20), was that sin might be defeated in its entirety. In His perfect life, He perfectly kept the law of God, all on our behalf. But then, at the Cross, He paid the penalty for sin, which was death, and did so by offering up His perfect life and perfect body, which completely made ineffective the sin nature, at least for those who will believe.

Listen again to Paul: *"Knowing this, that our old man* (what we were before salvation) *is crucified with Him* (when He died on the Cross, in the mind of God, we died with Him) *that the body of sin* (the sin nature, which came about as a result of the fall) *might be destroyed* (made inef-fective), *that henceforth we should not serve sin* (would not have to serve the sin nature)" (Rom. 6:3-6).

The word *destroyed* does not refer here to annihilation, but rather, that the sin nature is made, as stated, ineffec-tive. The secret is, we, as believers, as a result of the Cross, are to be dead to the sin nature (Rom. 6:11). It doesn't say that the sin nature is dead, but that we are to be dead unto that nature.

WHY IS THE SIN NATURE ITSELF NOT YET DEAD?

It is because our physical bodies are not yet redeemed.

Paul said: '*And not only they* (speaking of the creation), *but ourselves also* (all believers), *which have the firstfruits of the Spirit* (meaning that we do not have presently all that Jesus accomplished at the atonement, but only the firstfruits), *even we ourselves groan within ourselves, waiting for the adoption, to wit, the redemption of our body* (which will take place at the resurrection, i.e., the rapture of the church)' (Rom. 8:23).

At that time, our physical bodies will be glorified, and there will be no more sin nature.

Paul also said: '*So when this corruptible* (our present sta-tus) *shall have put on incorruption* (the glorified body), *and this mortal* (our physical bodies are now dying) *shall have put on immortality* (the glorified body will never die), *then shall be brought to pass the saying that is written, Death is swallowed up in victory'* (I Cor. 15:54).

The 'corruptible' pertains to the sin nature, which is still within us, even the godliest of believers. At the rapture of the church, there will be no more corruptible in the glorified body, which we will then receive.

But until then, the Lord has given us a means by which we can walk in victory in that the sin nature no longer rules or controls us in any fashion, which is done by our faith exclusively in Christ and what Christ has done for us at the Cross (Rom. 6:14).

THE LAST PUSH OF THE HOLY SPIRIT AS IT REGARDS THE CHURCH

It is my belief that the Holy Spirit bringing the church back to the Cross is the last great push that He will make before the rapture.

Those who look to Christ and the Cross, for Christ and the Cross must not be divided, will make up the true church. Those who reject the Cross, even though they may claim Christ in some manner, will be those who make up the apostate church. In fact, to accept Christ without the Cross is to accept *'another Jesus'* (II Cor. 11:4).

The Lord spoke to my heart, and I speak of the prayer meeting that I mentioned some paragraphs back, that He would begin a move in our particular church and ministry (Family Worship Center), which would girdle the globe. Of course, the Lord will be using many others, as well, but this ministry will definitely be a part of that which He is using.

He informed me that not only did I need, and desperately so, His help and grace, but, as well, the entirety of the church world fell into the same category. He showed me that by giving me, as stated, the words of Isaiah, which I quoted many paragraphs back.

That move began, at least as far as this ministry is concerned, in 1997. It began with the Message of the Cross. The church came in with the Cross, and the church will go out with the Cross. This means that the Lord has changed nothing, and simply because nothing needs to be changed. The Message of the Cross is *the everlasting covenant* (Heb. 13:20).

REFERENCES

CHAPTER 1

Frances Swaggart, "And Sarah Saw," *The Evangelist,* December 2015.

Frances & Friends, SonLife Broadcasting Network, September 28, 2015.

Jimmy Swaggart, *Jimmy Swaggart Bible Commentary, Galatians,* 342.

Gardiner Harris, David E. Sanger, and David M. Herszenhorn, "Obama Increases Number of Syrian Refugees for U.S. Resettlement to 10,000," *The New York Times,* September 10, 2015.

John Kerry: U.S. to Accept 85,000 Refugees in 2016, 100,000 in 2017, *Associated Press,* September 20, 2015.

Transcript: Read the Speech Pope Francis Gave to Congress, *Time Magazine,* September 24, 2015.

USAID Fact Sheet #8, FY 2015, September 21, 2015.

Josh Sanburn, "These 6 States Take in the Most Syrian Refugees," *Time Magazine*, September 10, 2015.

Susan Jones, "Counterterrorism Chair: We Have to Assume ISIS or Al Qaeda Would Try to Take Advantage of Refugee Situation," *CNSNews.com*, September 8, 2015.

Rep. Peter King, http://peteking.house.gov/issues/foreignaffairsdefense.

Neil Macdonald, "Why Barack Obama Won't Say 'Islamic Extremists': President Trying To Channel The Terror Debate A Certain Way, But Not Everyone Onside," *CBCnews*, February 27, 2015.

Snejana Farberov, "'We're Going To Be The Majority Soon!' Furious Muslim Parents Taunt New Jersey School Board Over Religious Holiday Closure," *Daily Mail*, September 23, 2015.

Thomas D. Williams, Ph.D., "7th Graders In Tennessee Made To Recite, 'Allah Is The Only God' In Public Schools", *Breitbart*, September 10, 2015.

"Do Muslims Believe Sharia Law Supersedes The Constitution?" Fox News, September 23, 2015, http://video.foxnews.com/v/4504765499001/do-muslims-believe-sharia-law-supersedes-the-constitution/?#sp=show-clips.

Lizzie Dearden, "David Cameron Extremism Speech: The PM Outlined Plans For A New Extremism Bill To Prevent Radicalisation," *Independent*, July 20, 2015.

Barack Obama, "Remarks by the President at the Summit on

Countering Violent Extremism." U.S. State Department, February 19, 2015.

CHAPTER 2

Frances Swaggart, "History Proves America Is Not A Muslim Nation," *The Evangelist*, March 2015.

CHAPTER 3

Frances Swaggart, "Enabling Evil" *The Evangelist*, March 2016.

CHAPTER 4

Frances Swaggart, "Communism" *The Evangelist*, August 2013.

Richard Wurmbrand, *Was Karl Marx a Satanist?* Diane Brooks Pub. Co., 1976, 6.

http://www.notablebiographies.com/Ma-Mo/Marx-Karl.html

Thomas Sowell, *Is Reality Optional?* Hoover Institution Press, 1993, 81.

CHAPTER 5

Frances Swaggart, "Conditioned For Communism" *The Evangelist*, November 2015.

Congressional Record, Appendix, pp. A34-A35, January 10, 1963.

Ali Meyer, "Food Stamp Beneficiaries Exceed 46,000,000 for

38 Straight Months," *CNSNews.com*, January 13, 2015.

Karl Marx and Frederick Engels, *Manifesto of the Communist Party*, February 1848, 39.

CHAPTER 6

Frances Swaggart, "Capitalism" *The Evangelist*, September 2013.

CHAPTER 7

Frances Swaggart, "Has Ethnic Loyalty In America Replaced Loyalty To Christ?" *The Evangelist*, June 2008.

http://www.tucc.org/about.htm.

http://www.tucc.org/about.htm.

http://www.trumpetmag.com/pdf/nov_dec_feature.pdf.

http://www.newswithviews.com/Daubenmire/dave108.htm.

CHAPTER 8

Frances Swaggart, "Common Core: Education Or Indoctrination?" *The Evangelist*, April 2016.

"Robert Muller, World Core Curriculum," http://robert-muller.org/rm/R1/World_Core_Curriculum.html.

"World Core Curriculum Home Page/Angela's Graduation Speech First Graduate & Valedictorian," http://www.worldcorecurriculum.org.

New Man Magazine, July-August 1995, 85-86.

Frances & Friends, SonLife Broadcasting Network, November 19, 2015.

"Common Core State Standards Initiative: Preparing America's Students For College & Career," http://www.corestandards.org/about-the-standards/frequently-asked-questions/.

Frances & Friends: The Truth About Common Core, 2014. DVD.

Valerie Strauss, "Everything You Need To Know About Common Core — Ravitch," *The Washington Post,* January 18, 2014.

"American Principles Project, Jane Robbins: Stop Common Core Series," https://americanprinciplesproject.org/education/jane-robbins-stop-common-core-series/.

"Dr. Sandra Stotsky on the Common Core National Education Standards," YouTube video, posted by Pioneer Institute, April 17, 2013, https://www.youtube.com/watch?v=-K4URgulWhk.

Kate Taylor, "English Class in Common Core Era: 'Tom Sawyer' and Court Opinions," *The New York Times,* June 19, 2015.

"Chinese American Mom: Common Core in U.S. Same As Communist Core in China," YouTube video, posted by Mert Melfa, November 14, 2014, https://www.youtube.com/watch?v=WAIetn6sE00.

"Stacie Starr: Lorain County Education Forum," YouTube video, posted by Toni J., February 10, 2015, https://www.youtube.com/watch?v=Hxtm7kogtgg.

"Robust Data Gives Us The Roadmap to Reform," U.S. Department of Education remarks delivered by Secretary

Arne Duncan, Fourth Annual IES Research Conference, June 8, 2009.

CHAPTER 9

Frances Swaggart, "Vain Imaginations" *The Evangelist,* September 2015.

Barack Obama, "Remarks by the President at LGBT Pride Month Reception," Washington, D.C. June 24, 2015.

Gary Levin, "Bruce Jenner Interview Scores Big Ratings," USA Today, April 26, 2015, http://www.usatoday.com/story/life/tv/2015/04/25/bruce-jenner-diane-sawyer-interview-abc-ratings/26361367/.

Diane Sawyer, "Bruce Jenner: The Interview," ABC News, 20/20, April 24, 2015, http://abc.go.com/shows/2020/listing/2015-04/24-bruce-jenner-the-interview.

"Injustice at Every Turn: A Report of the National Transgender Discrimination Survey," http://endtransdiscrimination.org/PDFs/NTDS_Exec_Summary.pdf.

Walt Heyer, "God Makes Male and Female," YouTube video, 1:29, posted May 23, 2014, https://www.youtube.com/watch?v=14o23J8A-u8.

Jimmy Swaggart, *Rape of a Nation,* Jimmy Swaggart Ministries, 1985, 152.

CHAPTER 10

Frances Swaggart, "Let No Man Put Asunder" *The Evangelist,* October 2015.

"Arlette Saenz, Same-Sex Ruling: President Obama's Historic Phone Call With Plaintiff Jim Obergefell," ABC News, June 26, 2015, http://abcnews.go.com/Politics/sex-ruling-president-obamas-historic-phone-call-plaintiff/story?id=32051689.

"Support for Same-Sex Marriage at Record High, but Key Segments Remain Opposed: 72 Percent Say Legal Recognition is 'Inevitable,'" Pew Research Center, June 8, 2015, http://www.people-press.org/files/2015/06/6-8-15-Same-sex-marriage-release1.pdf.

Heather Barwick, "Dear Gay Community: Your Kids Are Hurting," The Federalist, March 17, 2015, http://thefederalist.com/2015/03/17/dear-gay-community-your-kids-are-hurting/.

"Kirsten Andersen, 'Quartet of Truth': Adult Children Of Gay Parents Testify Against Same-Sex 'Marriage' at 5th Circuit," Life Site, January 13, 2015, https://www.lifesitenews.com/news/quartet-of-truth-adult-children-of-gay-parents-testify-against-same-sex-mar.

"Dawn Stefanowicz, My Father Was Gay. Why I Oppose Legalizing Same-Sex Marriage," The Daily Signal, April 13, 2015. http://dailysignal.com/print/?post_id=182334.

"Terrence P. Jeffrey, Alito Warns: Defenders of Traditional Marriage Now Risk Being Treated as Bigots by Governments, Employers, Schools," CNSNews.com, June 26, 2015, http://www.cnsnews.com/news/article/

terence-p-jeffrey/alito-warns-defenders-traditional-marriage-now-risk-being-treated.

Franklin Graham, Facebook post, June 29, 2015, https://www.facebook.com/FranklinGraham/posts/953210028068512.

CHAPTER 11

Frances Swaggart, "The Biblical View Of Homosexuality, Part I," *The Evangelist*, February 2013.

Aldous Huxley, *Brave New World*, (New York: HarperCollins, 1932), xvii .

"Berit Kjos, Warren's P.E.A.C.E. Plan and UN Goals–Part 3," September 2005, http://www.crossroad.to/articles2/05/peace-un-3.htm.

http://www.purposedriven.com/en-US/HIVAIDSCommunity/StartingAMinistry/Rainey_Ortberg_Blake_to_help_churches_at_upcoming_summit.htm.

CHAPTER 12

Frances Swaggart, "The Biblical View Of Homosexuality, Part III," *The Evangelist*, March 2008.

Dennis Prager, "Judaism's Sexual Revolution: Why Judaism (and then Christianity) Rejected Homosexuality." "Crisis" 11, no. 8 (September 1993).

Alan Sears & Craig Osten, *The Homosexual Agenda: Exposing the Principal Threat to Religious Freedom Today*, 27.

http://mccchurch.org/inside-mcc/

Katie Melone, "Leaving a Church Behind: Congregation Prepares for a New Beginning," *The Hartford Courant*, December 31, 2007, http://www.courant.com/news/local/lc/hc-episco1231.artdec31,0,4445062,story.

CHAPTER 13
Frances Swaggart, "The Dangers Of Alcohol, Part I," *The Evangelist*, March 2014.

CHAPTER 14
Frances Swaggart, "The Dangers Of Alcohol, Part II," *The Evangelist*, April 2014.

CHAPTER 15
Frances Swaggart, "Is There More Than One Way To God?" *The Evangelist*, February 2015.

http://www.jesus-is-savior.com/Wolves/oprah-fool.htm.

http://www.newswithviews.com/baldwin/baldwin409.htm.

http://www.rapidnet.com/~jbeard/bdm/exposes/graham/general.htm.

http://www.christianworldviewnetwork.com/article.php/3435/By_Brannon_Howse.

http://www.jesus-is-savior.com/Wolves/oprah-fool.htm.

CHAPTER 16
Frances Swaggart, "Spirits Of Light," *The Evangelist*, December 2013.

Encyclopedia Britannica, Vol. 15 (Encyclopedia Britannica, Inc., Chicago, 1968), 640.

Encyclopedia Britannica, Vol. 20 (Encyclopedia Britannica, Inc., Chicago 1968), 695.

Warren Smith, *The Light That Was Dark* (Conscience Press. Ravenna, Ohio, 2004), 16-17.

http://www.leaderu.com/orgs/probe/docs/eadie.html.

"Alice Bailey, From Bethlehem to Calvary," 153, http://www. av1611.org/kjv/mess_bible.html.

Godfre Ray King, *Unveiled Mysteries, ch. 1* (1934).

Neale Donald Walsch, *Conversations With God: an uncommon dialogue, book 1* (New York, G. P. Putnam's Sons, 1996), 1-2.

"Warren Smith, The Era of the Single Savior is Over — A New Age Peace Plan," http://www.lighthouse-trailsresearch. com/singlesavior.htm.

"Mike Oppenheimer, A Course In Miracles," http://www. letusreason.org/BookR3.htm.

Warren Smith, *Reinventing Jesus Christ, The New Gospel* (Conscience Press, 2002), 14-15.

http://www.crossroad.to/Excerpts/biblical-teaching/DeWaay. theophostics.htm.

"Leonard Sweet, Quantum Spirituality," 235, http://www. lighthousetrailsresearch.com/leonardsweet.htm.

"The Christ Light," http://www.souledout.org/christmaslight/ christmaslight.html.

"Cathy Burn, Masonic and Occult Symbols Illustrated," 27-28, http://www.seekgod.ca/msgdoctrine2.htm.

CHAPTER 17

Frances Swaggart, "He Opened To Us The Scriptures" *The Evangelist,* January 2016.

Frances & Friends, SonLife Broadcasting Network, October 13, 2015.

"A Conversation With Eugene Peterson, Author," 12th Annual Writer's Symposium By The Sea, February 23, 2007, https://www.youtube.com/watch?v=FaaIui7cESs.

NavPress, https://web.archive.org/web/20080819201637/ http://navpress.com/Message/HistoryAndFaqs/#11.

"Bible Research, Internet Resources for Students of Scripture"

http://www.bible-researcher.com/themessage.html.

Doug LeBlanc, "I Didn't Want to Be Cute," *Christianity Today 46/11,* October 7, 2002, 15.

Jimmy Swaggart, *Brother Swaggart, How Can I Understand The Bible?* (World Evangelism Press, 2009), 7-9.

Jimmy Swaggart, *25 Great Years...25 Anointed Sermons,* Jimmy Swaggart Ministries, 1981, 187-188.

CHAPTER 18

Frances Swaggart, "Grace Revolution Or Sin Revolution?" *The Evangelist,* June 2015.

CHAPTER 19

Frances Swaggart, "Spiritual Unity vs. Social Unity" *The Evangelist*, May 2012.

http://www.catholicnewsagency.com/new.php?n=11509.

Dave Hunt, "A Woman Rides the Beast." Internet video. http://video.aol.com/video-detail/a-woman-rides-the-beast-dave-hunt/1482438308.

"Roger Oakland, My Trip to the Rethink Conference," 2007 — http://www.understandthetimes.org/commentary/c73.shtml.

CHAPTER 20

Frances Swaggart, "A Conspiracy" *The Evangelist*, August 2012.
Warren interview with Charlie Rose, August 17, 2006.

CHAPTER 21

Frances Swaggart, "Matthew 24:14—For There Shall Arise False Christs, And False Prophets, And Shall Show Great Signs And Wonders; Insomuch That, If It Were Possible, They Shall Deceive The Very Elect," *The Evangelist*, March 2011.

CHAPTER 22

Frances Swaggart, "The Power Of The Spoken Word; Biblical Or Occult Law? Part V," *The Evangelist*, December 2008.
Jimmy Swaggart, *Hyper-Faith: A New Gnosticism?* (1982).

http://www.letusreason.org/Popteac37.htm.

http://www.letusreason.org/WF48.htm.

CHAPTER 23

Frances Swaggart, "The Rapture Of The Church," *The Evangelist*, March 2013.

CHAPTER 24

Frances Swaggart, "Christ Crucified by J. C. Ryle," *The Evangelist*, February 2014.

CHAPTER 25

Frances Swaggart, "The Message Of The Cross," *The Evangelist*, September 2011.

Jimmy Swaggart, *Jimmy Swaggart Bible Commentary*, Daniel, Chapter 7.